THINK & WRITE

Sequencing
Observing
Comparing
Classifying
Imagining
Evaluating

Activities for Grades 4-6

5889

 **Good Year Books**

are available for preschool through grade 12 and for every basic curriculum subject plus many enrichment areas. For more Good Year Books, contact your local bookseller or educational dealer. For a complete catalog with information about other Good Year Books, please write:

Good Year Books
Department GYB
1900 East Lake Avenue
Glenview, Illinois 60025

THINK & WRITE

Sequencing
Observing
Comparing
Classifying
Imagining
Evaluating

Activities for Grades 4-6

Hilarie N. Staton

Scott, Foresman and Company
Glenview, Illinois
Dallas, Texas   Oakland, New Jersey
Palo Alto, California   Tucker, Georgia
London

Acknowledgments

The author and publisher would like to thank the following for their helpful comments:

Loretta Wilson
David Yeager
Deborah Soglin
Dianne Weingardner
Jerold Kellman, Gabriel House

Contents

GET YOUR THOUGHTS IN ORDER

APPLES, ORANGES, AND "VROOTFRUITS"

NO PHONY BALONEY

Activities

Introduction

It's no secret that thinking skills have become a topic of concern among professional educators at every academic level: elementary, secondary, and college. Moreover, given the nature of the "information age" that is so quickly enveloping us, parents and children, employers and employees — even government leaders — are growing ever more cognizant of the critical need for students to learn how to think and express themselves clearly.

Combine this recent attention to thinking skills with the continuing concern about writing skills and you have the *raison d'etre* for **THINK & WRITE**. An activity book for grades 4 to 6, **THINK & WRITE** presents scores of activities designed to strengthen thinking skills — as those skills relate to written language — in the following areas: sequencing, observing, comparing, classifying, imagining, and evaluating.

Divided into three sections, **THINK & WRITE** follows a standard format in each *section*: introductory guidelines for the teacher followed by dozens of reproducible worksheets relating to the section topic. In addition, each *worksheet* also follows a standard format: a "THINK" section comes first, with a "WRITE" section immediately following. After students complete one worksheet, they will understand how to handle all the rest with little assistance required from the teacher.

The three sections —*GET YOUR THOUGHTS IN ORDER* (sequencing), *APPLES, ORANGES, AND "VROOTFRUITS"* (observing, comparing, classifying, and imagining), and *NO PHONY BALONEY* (evaluating) — are presented in annotated form in the Table of Contents. In addition to the worksheet title and page number, you'll find that each entry includes the cognitive skill emphasized in that activity.

Students will appreciate the enormous variety of **THINK & WRITE** activities. They will unscramble words and sentences, conduct surveys, create a treasure hunt, write a biography of a criminal, invent an imaginary animal, persuade voters to support their candidacy for office, compose an emotional "Ann Landers" letter, and much more. In fact, **THINK & WRITE** provides clear evidence that both thinking and writing can be a great deal of fun!

But these activities are just a starting point. They can and should be supplemented with thinking and writing activities drawn from the content areas. Equally important, they should function as a springboard to class brainstorming sessions, to sharing experiences that enrich both oral and writing skills, to learning that thinking and writing — though usually practiced in solitude — are part of the larger communication process by which humans transmit thoughts and feelings to each other. Writers need and must never forget their readers.

With its emphasis upon thinking skills that improve the organization, clarity, and impact of all written work, **THINK & WRITE** will make your students more aware of the bond between writers and readers — a delicate linkage that requires mutual effort and understanding if true communication is to exist.

GET YOUR THOUGHTS IN ORDER
Teacher's Guidelines: Sequencing

The activities in this section relate to sequencing. Sequencing puts thoughts in order, a necessity in writing if what appears on paper is to make sense. All writing must possess an overall structure that gives order — e.g., a time frame, logical development — and sentences and paragraphs must have their own well-developed sequence. Good writers often go back over their work, seeking to strengthen the structure and revising passages where the sequence could be expressed more clearly.

Students must be taught to organize (and reorganize!) their ideas and their words so that their papers achieve maximum coherence and clarity. Ideas must flow smoothly and culminate in a logical conclusion. To this end, students will find that they can alter any existing structure in their papers, play with a number of alternatives, and arrive at new sequences of words, sentences, and paragraphs that make better sense.

The following activities approach sequencing in several different ways. Here is a brief preview of the various ways the **THINK & WRITE** activities can help your students "get their thoughts in order."

Criteria Sequencing

Students need to learn that they can put the same material into an entirely different order by altering the sequencing criteria. Perhaps the best way to introduce criteria sequencing is to have the students organize themselves in a number of different ways: by height, by hair color, by birth date, etc. When they understand the concept, they can enjoy the criteria sequencing activities — "Next" and "Size, Color, And Speed."

You may want to expand upon these activities by turning your students loose in a brainstorming session. Have them develop lists of criteria by which animals, colors, noises, jobs, clothing, and other everyday items can be sequenced.

Ranking Sequencing

"E.T. For President!" and "That's the Pits!" are the **THINK & WRITE** activities that teach students to put likes and dislikes into a meaningful order. Although the ordering of our preferences is often unconscious, it is an integral part of our decision-making processes. Participating in a survey that requires the ranking of preferences is a good way to bring this thinking skill to the conscious level.

As follow-up to these activities, encourage students to pick a topic and develop their own lists for ranking, the actual ordering of items to be done by parents, peers, or the public in addition to themselves. Conducting a survey is a good small-group activity, especially if group members draw conclusions and judgments from the data they collect.

Letter And Word Sequencing

Activities involving scrambled words and sentences can make clear the importance of proper sequence to clear meaning. "Drmsbclae Orwsd (Scrambled Words)" and "Alphabet Soup" are **THINK & WRITE** activities in letter sequencing. You can use the same concept — putting letters in a specific order — to reinforce new vocabulary words in any subject area.

"Who Bit Whom?," "A Big Red Run," "The One With A Limp," "When?," "Finally!" and "Gobble De Gook," deal with word sequencing. Students work not only to keep meaning clear but also to keep sentences interesting as they learn the proper placement of modifiers (single words, phrases, and clauses) within a sentence.

Writing complex sentences that include adverbial clauses, for example, will help students recognize how important such clauses can be in denoting sequence. Writing the same basic sentence but shifting the position of the modifier will show students how varieties of word sequence can alter the tone and personality of their writing. "When?" and "Finally!" are activities that encourage variety in sentence composition by having students place adverbial modifiers in different locations.

Instructional And Routine Event Sequencing

Giving clear, concise directions is never easy. Students must learn how to describe a sequence of steps so that each item in the sequence is totally comprehensible in itself and so that the order of discrete steps leads smoothly from start to finish. "Do It My Way," "Building A Whatchamacallit," "Bake Me A Cake As Fast As You Can," "Over The River And Through The Woods," and "Pirate's Gold" provide practice in creating and sequencing step-by-step directions. "Garbage In The Refrigerator . . . Dinner Down The Drain" and "Every Day Is A Little Different And A Little The Same" reinforce the importance of proper sequence in describing commonplace events.

These activities also teach something else that good writers must keep in mind: Nothing is to be taken for granted. Writers must take care to provide every step in a sequence and to make certain that each step conveys all the information the reader needs to know.

Logical Sequencing

The **THINK & WRITE** logical sequencing activities — "If . . . Then . . . Oh, No!," "It Happened Because," and "It's Not My Fault" — teach cause/effect relationships as logically related sequences. Students should be encouraged to generate their own cause/effect situations and then develop those situations into stories. Alternative historical possibilities and scientific discoveries lend themselves especially well to if . . . then treatment.

Sentence And Paragraph Sequencing

Ordering ideas within sentences, sentences within paragraphs, and paragraphs within articles or stories is ultimately what sequencing in writing is all about. The final portion of GET YOUR THOUGHTS IN ORDER consists of activities that emphasize finding the main ideas ("Bare Bones"), putting those ideas into a well-organized outline ("How To Breathe Life Into A Skeleton"), reordering the ideas to create a different story ("The Spice Of Life"), constructing well-ordered paragraphs ("Smoothing the Ride" and "Let's Get One Thing Straight"), ordering paragraphs in a time sequence ("A Day In My Life"), and, finally, organizing chronological material into a brief biography ("A Life Of Crime").

Sequencing takes many forms, and often — in the hands of skilled writers — it is a very subtle art. Yet a comprehensible sequence must be present in everything we write. Learning a variety of ways to sequence will not only stretch a student's internal thought processes, but will also make him or her better able to communicate those thoughts to the outside world.

Next

THINK

Have you ever thought about all the different kinds of dogs in the world? They're all dogs, but they don't look or act the same. The dogs in the list below are arranged by size, starting with the biggest and going down to the smallest:

Saint Bernard
Dalmation
Spaniel
Toy Poodle
Chihuahua

Now, suppose you wanted to list the same dogs by the length of their hair, from longest to shortest. Your list would look like this:

Saint Bernard
Spaniel
Toy Poodle
Dalmation
Chihuahua

Both lists put the dogs in order, but they use different standards for judging the dogs. These standards are called "criteria." Here are some other criteria that you could use to list breeds of dogs: speed, friendliness, beauty, bark, color, and usefulness to people. Some criteria, like beauty, involve personal preference. Other criteria, like size, are based on objective measurements.

WRITE

In the space below, list as many animals (at least 20) as you can.

Now, list some criteria by which you could put a list of animals in order:

Pick one of the criteria and ten of the animals you listed. Think about the sequence — first, second, third, etc. — before you begin writing. Then list the animals in the proper order.

1. _____
2. _____
3. _____
4. _____
5. _____

6. _____
7. _____
8. _____
9. _____
10. _____

After you finish that list, pick another one of your criteria and make a new list so that the same animals appear in a different order.

1. _____
2. _____
3. _____
4. _____
5. _____

6. _____
7. _____
8. _____
9. _____
10. _____

Size, Color, And Speed

THINK

Imagine that you are in charge of an important auto race, the BUZZ 2000. It is your job to assign the starting positions. To figure out who goes where, use these three criteria IN THIS ORDER: 1. car speed 2. car size   3. car color.

The slowest cars go first. If two or more cars go the same speed, then the larger car goes first in its speed group. Finally, if cars have the same speed and size, then the car with the lighter color goes first.

Here are the cars entered in the BUZZ 2000. Arrange the lineup by putting the number of each car in its correct position.

Car Number	Trial Speed	Size	Color
1	150 m.p.h.	midsized	red
5	150 m.p.h.	sports	white
7	150 m.p.h.	sports	dark blue
2	200 m.p.h.	midsized	yellow
6	180 m.p.h.	midsized	yellow
3	183 m.p.h.	midsized	brown
4	160 m.p.h.	sports	light green
8	160 m.p.h.	sports	dark green
9	115 m.p.h.	fullsized	black
10	120 m.p.h.	midsized	brown

WRITE

Below you will find ten books that must be put on a shelf in some kind of order. Study the list. Develop three criteria that you could use to put the books in order. Decide how you can use all three criteria in one sequence.

Put the books in order using your different criteria. Remember, you must use all *three* criteria to create *one* sequence. When you find the solution, write the title and author's name on each book at the bottom of the page.

Author	Title	Illustrations	Fiction/Nonfiction
Hart, A.	*Rabbits and Bunnies*	Illustrated	Nonfiction
Hart, A.	*Dogs and Puppies*	Illustrated	Nonfiction
Hart, A.	*Rain Everywhere*	Not illustrated	Fiction
Jones, J.	*Covered Wagons*	Illustrated	Nonfiction
Jones, T.	*Clouds and Snow*	Illustrated	Nonfiction
Smith, C.	*Jane's Journey*	Not illustrated	Fiction
Brown, B.	*Mommy'sMoney*	Illustrated	Fiction
Turner, T.	*Timothy Turtle*	Illustrated	Fiction
Zip, M.	*Pioneers*	Not illustrated	Nonfiction
Abbot, Q.	*The Quiet Man*	Illustrated	Fiction

E.T. For President!

THINK

You can learn a great deal about people by conducting a survey. A survey can tell you about their likes and dislikes. Some surveys ask people to list likes and dislikes in order, putting the most liked thing on top of the list and the least liked at the bottom.

Look at the three lists below. For each list, put your favorite (#1) at the top, followed by your next choice (#2), with your least favorite choice (#3) last.

A. For president, I'd vote for: E.T., Superman, James Bond.

1. _____
2. _____
3. _____

B. Around the house, I'd pick these chores: take out the garabage, clean my room, wash the dishes.

1. _____
2. _____
3. _____

C. If I had great news, the first person I'd tell would be a: parent, teacher, friend.

1. _____
2. _____
3. _____

You can learn something about how your class thinks by making a tally sheet like the one below for each survey list.

Survey A

	1	2	3
E.T.	_____	_____	_____
Superman	_____	_____	_____
James Bond	_____	_____	_____

Put the number of 1's, 2's, and 3's your class gave each choice on the appropriate line. Then examine the tally sheet. Discuss the reasons why certain choices were popular. Think about other choices you could ask people to list in order.

WRITE

Now it is your turn to develop a survey. Write six questions about one subject (movies, people, feelings, hobbies, and so forth). Each question should have three choices for answers. Ask ten to fifteen people to put the choices in order for each question. Tally the answers, and study your results.

Finally, write two paragraphs about the choices that people made. Be sure to include your own ideas about why people put certain choices at the top of their lists and others at the bottom.

_____
_____
_____
_____
_____
_____
_____
_____
_____
_____
_____
_____
_____
_____
_____
_____
_____
_____

(continue on another sheet of paper)

That's The Pits!

THINK

Everyday, we sequence things without even thinking much about them. We list our favorite music, foods, and books or the vegetables we hate. We decide which TV shows are great, OK, or terrible. It's natural to put things in some kind of order in our minds.

Look at the lists below. Put each list in order by numbering the items. Start with "1" for the item you like best, and order the rest down to "5" for the one you like least. Actually, you may not like any of them — or you may like all of them — but you must put them in order. You have to make a choice!

Colors

_____ red

_____ green

_____ yellow

_____ blue

_____ purple

Vegetables

_____ peas

_____ spinach

_____ squash

_____ lettuce

_____ broccoli

Activities

_____ drawing

_____ writing

_____ cooking

_____ reading

_____ riding bikes

Now list the things you REALLY hate! Start with the worst thing next to number 1 in each category; number 2 should be something that is a little better; and 3 something that is barely OK.

Chores

1._____

2._____

3._____

Places

1._____

2._____

3._____

Punishments

1._____

2._____

3._____

WRITE

Write down the following items from your lists:

    #1 punishment _____

    #2 chore _____

Add a place that you have always wanted to go _____

Use the above information to write a short story. The story should describe how you get (or don't get) to the place you want because of your #2 chore and your #1 punishment — or threat of that punishment.

_____

_____

(continue on another sheet of paper)

Drmsbclae Orwsd
(Scrambled Words)

THINK

It's easy to figure out scrambled words when you know the way the letters should be put in sequence. For example, you can quickly discover these mystery words just by putting the letters in alphabetical order:

telb _____   pymet _____   sfitr _____

yjo _____   smot _____   zcinht _____

wonk _____   opcy _____   qsecunee _____

A clue about a word can help you figure out the letter sequence. For example, it won't take you long to sequence the letters "s o c e r o r i h n" once you know that the letters spell the name of a big animal.

Figure out the scrambled words below by using the clues.

g l e c n e a r t (a shape) _____

t i r u f (a kind of food) _____

s a d i y (the name of a flower) _____

WRITE

Write a message about what you are planning to do after school today. Then think of a sequence rule (like alphabetical order, letter height, or meaning clues) that you can use to scramble every word in your message. Exchange scrambled messages with a friend. See who can be the first to figure out the sequence rule and decode the scrambled message.

_____

_____

_____

(continue on another sheet of paper)

Alphabet Soup

THINK

Look at these two bowls of alphabet soup. Each bowl is loaded with letters. Under each bowl are two ways you can sequence the letters. Each way will put the letters in a different order. Put the letters in order according to each set of instructions.

1. alphabetical order

2. order in which these letters appear in the next paragraph.

1. reverse (backwards) alphabetical order

2. order in which these letters spell phrase about a butcher's tool.

The cups of alphabet soup below contain letters that spell actual words. Sequence each cup's letters first by letter height. Start with letters that reach below the line. Then go on to letters that do not reach either below or above the line. Finally, do the letters that reach above the line. When you find more than one letter in the same height group, sequence by alphabetical order. You must follow this two-part sequence to get the *correct* word.

WRITE

Now it is your turn to make some alphabet soup. Try to think of some unusual ways to sequence letters. Remember, the alphabet is just one of many ways you can sequence letters. Put each set of scrambled letters in a soup bowl. Then, below each bowl, describe the way to sequence the letters inside. The letters do not have to spell a real word when put in the right order. For at least one bowl, suggest two different ways to sequence the letters.

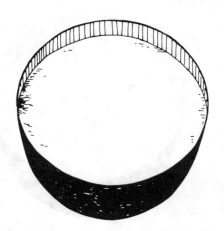
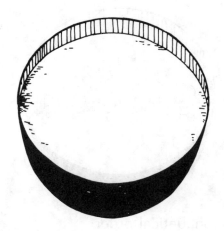

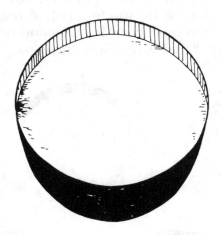
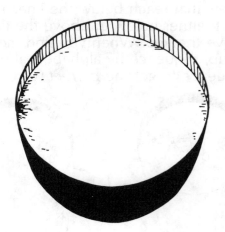

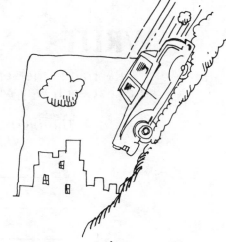

Who Bit Whom?

THINK

Just by changing the order of words in a sentence, you can change the whole meaning. Sometimes the sentence can end up sounding silly. Sometimes it will make better sense. Sometimes the new sentence will make the action sound more exciting. Sometimes, though, changing the order of words in a sentence can cause a real misunderstanding.

For example:

John chased the dog across the road.
The dog chased John across the road.

Either sentence could be true, but the meaning of each is totally different.

Here are some other examples:

The big car raced down the mountainside toward the city.
The big city raced down the car toward the mountainside.
Down the mountainside, toward the big city, raced the car.

One of these sentences makes no sense, but two of them do. Of the two that make sense, which one seems more exciting? Which one creates a clearer picture of the action in your mind? Writers often change the sequence of words in sentences in order to make readers see and feel things a little differently.

WRITE

Rearrange the sentences below two or three different ways, but be sure that each way MAKES SENSE.

The big black dog snarled and snapped at whatever was hiding in the shadows.

_____

_____

_____

_____

_____

The fast, shiny train trailed smoke as it raced across the dry, brown plains.

_____

_____

_____

_____

_____

Wonderful aromas came from the hot steamy kitchen where Nora cooked.

_____

_____

_____

_____

_____

Now write several sentences of your own. Rearrange each one at least once. Try to get different meanings by moving single words and whole phrases. See if you can make a sentence sound more exciting just by changing its word sequence.

_____

_____

_____

(continue on another sheet of paper)

A Big Red Run

THINK

You can make sentences more interesting by adding words that describe things and actions. You MUST choose these words carefully, however. And you MUST put them in the right places.

Think about this sentence:

The dog howled.

A few descriptive words can make it much more interesting.

The dirty, sick, deserted dog often howled with loneliness.

The same words, though, can turn the sentence into a mess if you put them in the wrong order.

The often loneliness dog with dirty, sick, deserted and howled.

Use descriptive words to fill in the blanks in the sentences below. Make sure that your new words make sense.

His _____ _____ clothes fit him _____

The _____ _____ hill looked _____ steep.

She _____ picked _____ , _____ , _____ flowers.

WRITE

Pretend that you have just walked into each of the following places for the first time. Tell what each one looks like in three or four clear, descriptive sentences. Imagine you are speaking into your secret spy transmitter. Don't try to tell everything. You don't have time. Be as clear as possible by using a few of the best words you can think of to describe each place.

1. Your bedroom.

_____

_____

_____

_____

_____

2. The school office.

_____

_____

_____

_____

_____

3. An amusement park.

_____

_____

_____

_____

_____

The One
With A Limp

THINK

A phrase is a group of related words. It can be used to add description. A phrase usually describes the word just before or after it.

"A girl went by" is a simple sentence. "A girl, the one with a limp, went by" is a more descriptive sentence. It contains a phrase that gives the reader a better picture of the girl. "A girl, the one with a limp, went by in a big hurry" tells you even more. It contains two descriptive phrases.

Below you will find two simple sentences and several phrases. Rewrite each sentence twice. Use different phrases each time to create different pictures. Be sure to put the phrase in the right place for the sentence to make sense. Remember, a phrase usually describes the word just before or just after it.

The monster went hunting.

1. _____

2. _____

The lady greeted her guests.

1. _____

2. _____

Phrases: dripping green slime   near the loose rocks
with a broad sword   with fuzzy, silver fur
who had pale blue skin   under a bright purple awning

Did you add more than one phrase to some sentences? Did you put the phrases in different parts of the sentences?

WRITE

Now it is your turn to use your imagination. Add descriptive phrases wherever you see an asterisk (*) in the sentences below. Write the new sentence, and then reread it to make sure it makes sense.

*The * spaceship landed **

_____

*The astronaut * came out * .*

_____

*A * alien * appeared * .*

_____

*** rain began * .*

_____

*The * ground shook * .*

_____

Now, try to build sentences around each of these five words. Include at least one phrase in each sentence. Remember, a phrase is a group of related words that usually describes the word just before or just after it.

rocks

_____

watched

_____

lifted

_____

sun

_____

quiet

_____

18

When?

THINK

Adverbs are words that tell you something more about the verbs, adjectives, or even other adverbs in a sentence. They can be very handy in giving a sense of time or order to your writing.

Look at the sentence below:

After Mary gets back, we'll have a party.''

''After'' is the adverb that tells the order. It tells the reader: First, Mary has to get back. Second, there will be a party.

Here's another sentence for you to examine:

The party began as soon as Mary arrived.

In this sentence, ''as soon as'' is an adverbial phrase that tells the reader: First, Mary arrived. Then the party started.

Notice that the adverb or adverbial phrase can be at the beginning, middle, or end of the sentence. It can tell what will happen first, second, or even at the same time. You must be careful, of course, to put the events in the right order when you are using adverbs.

Read each of the sentences below. Then list the order of the events in each one.

Take out the garbage before you go to school.

    First:

    Second:

Zack will be punished as soon as his father gets home.

    First:

    Second:

Although Jane arrived early, the bus had left already.

    First:

    Second:

WRITE

Pretend that you are a movie star. Write a paragraph of at least eight sentences about an ordinary day in your life. Be sure to use adverbs and adverbial phrases — "after," "before," "lately," "as soon as," "until," "first," etc. — to tell the reader the order of events. Try to use a variety of words and phrases. And be sure to put these words and phrases in different parts of your sentences. If you use the sequence word at the beginning or end of every sentence, your story can become boring. Don't make your movie star's life boring!

A Star's Day

_____
_____
_____
_____
_____
_____
_____
_____
_____
_____
_____
_____
_____
_____
_____
_____
_____
_____

(continue on another sheet of paper)

Finally!

THINK

A clause is part of a sentence with its own subject and verb. A clause can act as an adverb to help tell a sequence of events. You can place these clauses in different spots in a sentence. For instance:

*The brown fox hid **until the hunter passed by.***
***After the hunter passed by,** the fox came out of hiding.*
*The tricky fox, who always hid **before the hunter saw him,**
crept down the road.*

The sentence parts in bold type are adverbial clauses. To make your writing more interesting, try putting adverbial clauses in different places in your sentences.

WRITE

A magazine editor has assigned you to write an article about an exciting adventure. Make up at least two characters, and have the action take place at an unusual location (jungle, desert, island, etc.). Describe the location fully, and involve your characters in several events.Use adverbial clauses to keep the sequence of events clear. And keep your writing interesting by putting the clauses in different parts of your sentences.

Characters:

Location:

Events:

_____

_____

_____

_____

_____

_____

(continue on another sheet of paper)

Gobble
De Gook

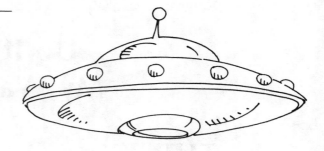

THINK

You are very lucky. You have been chosen to greet the latest visitors from outer space. The aliens have landed and sent a message. You must practice their language and then send a message back to them. The aliens use the same words we do, but they put the words in a different order to make their sentences. To understand what the aliens are saying, you must reorder their words. Translate these sentences to discover why the visitors have come to Earth.

EARTH ON HELLO PEOPLE!

_____

URANUS LITTLE THE WE PEOPLE BLUE ARE OF!

_____

come peace in we.

_____

help we need your!

_____

used need planet's our live we up salt and it to we.

_____

trade for please gold us salt.

_____

gold of we plenty have.

_____

WRITE

Now develop a greeting with which to welcome the aliens in their language. Trade greetings with a classmate, and see if you can translate each other's messages.

Greeting

_____

_____

(continue on another sheet of paper)

Do It
My Way

THINK

Our daily activities can be broken down into a series of steps. Sometimes we must do the steps in a particular order. At other times, we can pick our own order.

For example, when you set the table, you can lay down the forks first or the spoons first. The choice between laying out the spoons or the forks is a preference (the way you like to do something). It is not critical which you do first. What is critical is that you bring the forks or spoons to the table before you can put them in the right spots. That MUST be done. It is a CRITICAL step. You have no choice in a critical step. You must do it in the correct sequence or something will go wrong.

Read these sentences about a daily activity. Number the sentences in the order that you would do them.

_____ Put peanut butter on one piece of bread.

_____ Put jelly on one piece of bread.

_____ Take out two pieces of bread, a knife, the peanut butter and jelly.

Go back and decide if there is a critical step. Put a "C" after the step that must be done at a particular point in the sequence.

WRITE

Here are some critical steps and the activities to which they belong. Pick one critical step and list at least two more steps in the activity. Be sure to make the action in each step clear and to put all the steps in the proper sequence.

1. Turn on the oven (baking).
2. Take off the cap from the toothpaste (brushing teeth).
3. Look both ways for oncoming cars (crossing a street).
4. Open the chimney flue (building a fire in the fireplace).

Look over your steps and think what would happen if you changed the order of the critical step. Imagine the funny or sad or disastrous results. Write a short story about the time someone did the critical step out of sequence.

_____

_____

(continue on another sheet of paper)

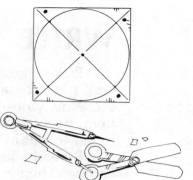

Building A Whatchamacallit

THINK

Picture in your mind a home on Christmas Eve. Under the big decorated tree are piles of presents. The children are asleep in their beds. The adults, though, are struggling to put together a bike and a dollhouse. They are struggling because the directions are poorly written.

Directions need to be clear and precise or else the results are likely to be a disaster. Read these directions, and then try to follow them.

1. Draw lines and a circle on your paper.
2. Cut along the lines to the circle.
3. Bend the corners.
4. Pin the paper to a pencil.

Any luck? If not, start over with the directions below.

1. Gather these materials: stiff paper, tape, a ruler, a pencil with an eraser, scissors, a straight pin, and a compass (or a circle with a 1/2-inch diameter).
2. Measure and draw a seven-inch square on the stiff paper. Cut out the square.
3. Set the compass for 1/4 inch. This will give you a circle with a 1/2-inch diameter. Draw the circle on another piece of stiff paper. Mark the center of the circle, and cut the circle out.
4. Lay the ruler on the square so that it goes from one corner to the opposite corner through the center. Draw a line along the ruler.
5. Repeat step 4 for the other two corners. Your square should now look like this:

6. Look at the square. Note the four triangles it contains. Put a dot in the lower right-hand corner of the bottom triangle. Place a dot in the same location in each of the other triangles. Your square should now look like this:

7. Match the center of the circle with the center of the square. Trace around the circle onto the square.
8. Starting at each corner of the square, cut toward the center along the lines you drew. Stop at the circle you traced. STOP! Don't cut into the circle. Make sure you cut all four corners the same way.
9. Gently curl each corner with a dot in it toward the center of the square. BE CAREFUL NOT TO CREASE FOLDS INTO THE PAPER! Match the dots to the center dot. Tape down all the corners in the center.
10. Push the straight pin through the center of the circle. Then push the pin through the square where all the dots meet. Be sure you catch all four taped-down corners with the pin.
11. Now push the pin, with the paper on it, firmly into the pencil's eraser.
12. Blow on the paper and watch the pinwheel spin.

WRITE

Pick something you can make without having directions in front of you. It can be a paper airplane, a paper snowflake, a woven placemat, etc. Now write out directions so that someone else can make the same item. Be sure you include every step in the correct sequence. Don't forget to put in any helpful warnings or hints.

Reread your directions to make certain they are as clear as they can be. Then give your directions to someone else in class. That person should be able to make the item quickly and easily by following your directions. If the other person runs into trouble, check to see if the problem is due to unclear or poorly sequenced directions.

(continue on another sheet of paper)

Bake Me
A Cake
As Fast
As You Can

THINK

Have you ever seen someone get angry while cooking because he or she couldn't understand the recipe? Just about everyone who cooks has come upon a recipe that is hard to follow. The reason may be because the directions are not clear, the critical steps are in the wrong sequence, or something important has been left out.

Here is a list of hints for writing recipe directions:

1. List each item (ingredients, bowls, etc.) needed.
2. Put the directions in the correct order. Note the critical steps.
3. Take out any extra words. Tell exactly what to do, but keep directions as brief as possible.
4. Explain terms. Many recipes assume you know special words and methods. Don't assume; EXPLAIN!
5. Give advance warning about any possible dangers or steps that require special care.

Look through several cookbooks to see how well they follow these rules.

WRITE

Create your own recipe for an imaginary cake. Include all of the normal ingredients — flour, salt, milk, baking soda, and sugar — but add something unusual to flavor it. You might also want to include decorating and serving suggestions.

When writing your recipe, keep in mind the rules you just learned about good directions. Don't forget to mention pan size, oven temperature, how to test the cake, and how to take it out of the pan. Watch the sequence of steps. You may include some silly ingredients, but make all the steps logical.

Over The River
And
Through The Woods

THINK

Stop and think about all the times you have used directions to get someplace. You may have used directions that were written down, or you may have followed the route that someone told you. The best directions are clear, as short as possible, and list clues and landmarks to help you keep track of your progress.

Here is a map. It shows Gwendolyn's house and her grandmother's house. Gwendolyn and her father are taking the horse and sleigh for a ride over the river and through the woods to go to grandmother's house for Thanksgiving dinner. Neither her father nor the horse knows the way. Gwendolyn must give directions as they go along.

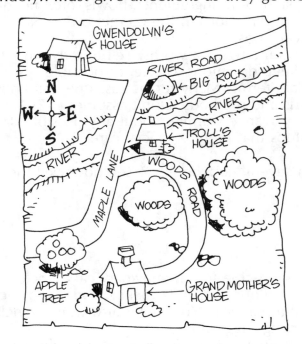

WRITE

Study the map. Then decide which route they should take. Write out the directions Gwendolyn must give to her father. Be sure to tell where they must turn, which direction to head (right, left, north, south, etc.), and what landmarks they should see along the way. Be clear and brief, but include enough details so that they can figure out if they are on the right route.

This Is The Way To Grandmother's House

_____

_____

(continue on another sheet of paper)

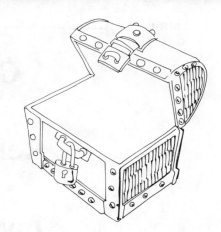

Pirate's Gold

THINK

You must hide this treasure chest. But first, fill the chest by coloring in your dream treasure. Then cut it out, and decide where you want to hide it. Keep in mind, though, that your partner — NOT YOU — is going to have to recover it.

WRITE

Write out a set of directions to get to your hidden treasure chest. Do not actually say where the chest is located. You can tell which way to turn, how many steps to take, what to look under, even which room to go to. Include at least ten steps in your directions. Make sure that each step is so clear that there will be no misunderstanding.

The goal of the Pirate Writer (you) is to write directions so clear that the Pirate Partner (the person following your written directions) can figure out exactly where the treasure is hidden. The goal of the Pirate Partner is to follow each step exactly as it is written and then to locate the chest.

The Pirate Writer must not give any hints or answer any questions. The Pirate Partner must not guess where the treasure is hidden. He or she must find it by following the step-by-step directions.

_____

_____

_____

_____

_____

_____

_____

_____

(continue on another sheet of paper)

Garbage In
The
Refrigerator…
Dinner
Down The Drain

THINK

Have you ever had "one of those days" when every little thing goes wrong? You put on socks of two different colors. The dog gets tangled up in his leash and knocks over the garbage can — full, of course. You make the bed, but then see a big lump where your little brother left his teddy bear. Finally, you leave for school only to realize that you forgot to put the peanut butter in your peanut butter and jelly sandwich.

Some of these problems are the result of forgetting a step in an activity or putting the steps in the wrong order. Often these problems are very frustrating to you but very funny to your friends when you describe "one of those days."

WRITE

Write a funny short story about someone who is having "one of those days." Tell about just one part of the day, but include at least four things that go wrong. Make sure that some of these events result from steps that are missing or out of order. Make up an interesting

Before you begin writing, list each disaster and what it does to your sequence of events. Have a final scene where something finally goes right, the character gives up, or a final disaster occurs.

One Of Those Days

_____

_____

_____

_____

_____

_____

 (continue on another sheet of paper)

Every Day Is A Little Different And A Little The Same

THINK

Usually we don't think about the steps that make up daily tasks. Routines like brushing our teeth, washing our hair, making a sandwich, or clearing the table seem to be just single events. But each of these tasks consists of many separate steps that we must do in the right order if we are to be successful.

Think about the steps involved in brushing your teeth.

1. Walk over to the sink.
2. Pick up the toothpaste tube.
3. Unscrew the top. Put the top down on the edge of the sink.
4. Pick up your toothbrush.
5. Turn on the cold water, and hold the brush's bristles under the running water.
6. Squeeze the toothpaste tube gently while pointing its open end toward the bristles. Squeeze out just enough tooothpaste to cover the bristles.
7. Replace the top on the tube, and set the tube down on the edge of the sink.
8. Place the bristles of the brush against your teeth and move it back and forth. (You can even break down your brushing motion into several steps.)
9. Spit out some of the toothpaste into the sink.
10. Rinse off your toothbrush and hang it up.
11. Fill a glass with water.
12. Take a mouthful of water and swish it around your mouth.
13. Spit out the water.
14. Repeat steps 12 and 13 until your mouth feels clean.
15. Empty the glass and rinse the sink.
16. Turn off the water.
17. Replace the glass in its proper slot.
18. Pick up the towel.
19. Dry your face and hands on the towel, and then replace the towel on the rack.

WRITE

Now *you* pick a routine task. Break it down into its smaller steps. Be sure to list every step. And make certain that you put all the steps in the right order.

You can pick any task you like, but here are a few suggestions: feeding a pet, checking out a book at the library, boiling an egg, making your bed.

Task:

Step 1. _____

Step 2. _____

Step 3. _____

Step 4. _____

Step 5. _____

Step 6. _____

Step 7. _____

Step 8. _____

Step 9. _____

THE YEAR IS 1620...

If...
Then...
Oh, No!

THINK

Imagine what would have happened if a radio news team had been on hand as Columbus landed in America or as the founding fathers signed the Declaration of Independence. What would the reporters have said about the event? Whom would they have interviewed?

Here's an example of what a radio news broadcast might have sounded like at one famous historic event:

"The year is 1620, and it is a bitterly cold December day. We are looking out over the Atlantic Ocean. A ship is just arriving. I can barely make out its name. . . . The . . . Mayflower. Yes, that's it. Now, a rowboat full of men is landing near a large rock. The men look pale and tired. They are all dressed in dark clothing. Here comes one of the men. Perhaps he can tell us more.

"Excuse me, sir, please tell our audience who you are and why you have come here."

"My name is William Bradford, and we are the Pilgrims. We have been searching for religious freedom. We have come to the New World to worship as we wish."

"And there you have it. The Pilgrims have landed at Plymouth Rock. They will have to build homes, plant crops, and try to get along with the Indians. Some will die during hard times ahead, but more settlers will come in the future. Perhaps they truly will make this a country where people can worship freely. I wish them luck. . . . And now, back to you, Fred.

WRITE

Now it is your turn to write a radio news broadcast about a famous event in history. Follow these guidelines:

1. Pick an event, and list everything you know about it.
2. Research the people, places, and actions involved.
3. Evaluate your facts, and choose the important ones.
4. Think about the related events that came after the one you picked. You can make some predictions, but be sure you have reasons for mentioning later events in your broadcast.
5. Write an interesting broadcast that covers the people, places, and actions. Be sure to include some related future events. Your broadcast should last from one to three minutes.

_____

_____

(continue on another sheet of paper)

It Happened
Because

THINK

You can write anything from short sentences to long stories with a "cause-and-effect" theme. The cause makes the effect (or result) happen. Sometimes the cause is clear, but often it is hidden. Effects are usually easier to tell, but they, too, may not be obvious.

Although the cause always happens before the effect in time sequence, it may not come first in a sentence. The sentences below show how cause and effect can come in different order.

> *John got scared* [effect] *when he saw the wolf stalking the lamb* [cause].
> *Sally saw the birthday cake* [cause] *and grinned* [effect].
> *The plants were wilted* [effect] *because they had no water* [cause].
> *The long, hot, dry summer* [cause] *had turned many lawns brown* [effect].

See if you can place "cause" or "effect" correctly in these sentences.

> *He poured a green liquid into the bowl* [   ], *turning the contents blue* [   ].
> *School closed early* [   ] *because a severe storm was approaching* [   ].
> *Due to the light gravity on the moon* [   ], *the astronauts moved quickly across the barren plain* [   ].
> *Dogs grow thick coats* [   ] *when the weather turns colder* [   ].

WRITE

Writing about science topics often involves cause-and-effect sentences. Pick one of the science topics listed below and write ten sentences about it. Make most of them cause-and-effect sentences.

Topics

Animals And The Seasons

Traveling In Space

Simple Machines That Work Hard

Weather And Plants

The Earth Moves

Staying Healthy

It's Not My Fault

THINK

Have you ever been accused of causing a disaster that you had nothing to do with? Many people tend to get confused about "causes" and "effects" (results). Just because one thing happened before another doesn't mean that the first thing caused the second. And to make the whole situation even more confusing, many effects have more than one cause!

Think about this sentence:

The baby was crying because _____ .

You could complete that sentence with any of the following reasons:

her diaper was wet.   *her rattle fell.*
she was hungry.   *she was tired.*
a bug was bothering her.   *she wanted to play.*

Each would be a good guess as to why the baby was crying.

Sentences that tell about causes and effects often contain such keys words as "because," "so," etc. Use key words where necessary as you fill in the blanks below. See how many causes you can think of for each sentence.

Betty _____ , so she threw the book at him.

_____ , causing Dick to land on the ground.

All the money was gone _____ .

Tears flowed down her wrinkled face _____ .

WRITE

Small children like to hear stories about someone searching for an answer. You are going to write a search story for first graders. It will be a story that involves cause and effect.

First, pick an effect that would appeal to a little boy or girl — a broken toy, a missing pet, a sick child, and so forth. Then invent a main character who will search for the cause. This character need not be a person. It could be an animal. Write your choices here.

Effect:

Main Character:

List all the crazy and not so crazy causes for your effect. Add or eliminate some so that you have about eight or ten. Make notes about other characters who will deny being the cause. For instance, if you picked a broken toy, you might have the cat deny knocking the toy off the shelf.

Possible Causes:

Who And How Denied:

Finally, pick the real cause and decide how your main character will discover it. Remember, you are writing for young children, so make the action interesting to them.

Real Cause:

How Discovered:

Now, write a story that begins with the main character discovering the effect. Follow his search through several possible but incorrect causes. End with him finding the correct cause. Don't use too many words. Remember, this is a story for little kids. Make sure they will enjoy both the search and the cause you have chosen.

Who Did It?

_____

_____

_____

(continue on another sheet of paper)

Smoothing The Ride

THINK

Sometimes, especially when something exciting happens, we have so much to say that we don't tell our story clearly. If we are writing the story, we have a chance to cut out the confusion by putting the sentences in better order.

Look at the story Tom wrote about his trip to Los Angeles. Read it carefully, and then renumber the sentences in each paragraph. Make the story flow better.

My Trip

_____ It was a long flight. _____ The lights looked like twinkling stars in the sky. _____ Mother woke me as we were coming in for a landing. _____ The plane arrived at night.

_____ I got a bad case of sunburn. _____ The next day we slept late. _____ The sun was very hot, and the sand burned my feet. _____ Then we went to the beach.

_____ Space Mountain was scary. _____ Even though I felt sick and sore, I wanted to go. _____ The next day we were supposed to go to Disneyland. _____ The Jungle Cruise was fun. _____ Mom bought me a hat to protect my burned face. _____ I even got to drive a car by myself. _____ I'd go back in a minute.

WRITE

Pick a place you've always wanted to go. If you don't know much about the place, do some research to find out about it. You are going to write a letter to a friend back home describing your wonderful trip.

Your letter should have at least ten sentences. Put the sentences into several paragraphs, and make sure each paragraph has a topic sentence. Describe the place you are visiting, and add some personal information about your adventures there.

Reread the letter to make sure each paragraph makes sense and that the whole letter flows smoothly. Then copy it over in correct letter form.

_____

_____

_____

(continue on another sheet of paper)

Let's Get
One Thing Straight

THINK

Writers often start with what they call a "first draft." They write down all their thoughts just to get their ideas on paper. Later, they rearrange their ideas to make better sense. They switch sentences around within a paragraph, and they even move sentences from one paragraph to another. They try to make their thoughts as clear as possible to their readers.

You can improve many paragraphs simply by rearranging the sentences. Read the paragraph below. Then number the sentences to show how a different sequence could make a better paragraph.

_____ Pinball machines have been around since the early 1930's. _____ This did not stop the companies from producing the games. _____ Today, Gottlieb and Bally are still manufacturing pinball games in Chicago. _____ They were located in Chicago. _____ From the 1930's until 1976, however, playing pinball was illegal in Chicago. _____ Gottlieb and Bally were the first companies to make pinball machines.

WRITE

Maria had 1,001 excuses for not doing her homework. The excuses just seemed to pour out of her. Her teacher asked Maria to write down the reasons so that they would be less confusing. You can help Maria by rewriting her excuses in a way that makes better sense.

I didn't get home until 12 o'clock. My brother leaves for the army tomorrow. I did the food shopping for my mother at the all-night grocery store. Every afternoon I clean Mrs. Jones' house. He needed clean clothes so I had to do the laundry. Since she was giving a dinner party, I had to stay late. I was so tired that I fell asleep over my books.

What Maria is trying to say is

_____

_____

_____

_____

_____

(continue on another sheet of paper)

Punch Lines

THINK

Something is wrong. The words don't go with the pictures. The dialog is out of order, and the comic strip makes no sense. Reorder the dialog and write it in the balloons below so that the "punch line," or joke, comes at the end.

WRITE

Write you own dialog for the comic strip below. Make sure the dialog goes with the picture. Remember to put the punch line last.

Bare Bones

THINK

Do you realize how important it is to find the main ideas every time you read an article in a newspaper or magazine? Get one of your favorite magazines, and pick out an article that is (1) nonfiction; (2) short but has at least three paragraphs; and (3) about a person rather than an event.

Skim the article. Then go back and read it slowly. As you read each paragraph, write down its main idea. Use only a *few* words. Do not include all the details.

Main Ideas

WRITE

Use the main ideas you found in the article to write a summary paragraph. Begin your summary with a topic sentence that mentions the name of the magazine and article. Do not include details, but be sure to express each main idea in a good sentence. Finish your summary with a statement of your feelings about this article.

_____

_____

_____

_____

(continue on another sheet of paper)

How To
Breathe
Life
Into A Skeleton

THINK

When you begin writing, you must decide what main ideas you want to cover. Those main ideas are your topics. You can use those main ideas to create an outline. An outline is the skeleton for what you want to write.

To fill in the outline, you add details. Details make your ideas clearer. They are the flesh and blood of your writing. The actual words you choose and the order you put those words in give your writing its "personality" or life. Below are some main ideas you can use for an essay on an animal — ANY animal! Decide which animal you want to write about. Research that animal with these main ideas in mind. Collect as many details as you can find.

Main Ideas: environment, food, activities, physical description, babies.

Details:

When you finish the research, organize your main ideas on the outline form below. Put each main idea next to a Roman numeral. Then, under each main idea, list the details you learned from your research.

I.

II.

III.

IV.

V.

WRITE

When you have a complete outline with enough details, write the essay. Each main idea should be a paragraph in your essay. Make sure that each paragraph has a topic sentence and plenty of details to support the main idea.

Essay — First Draft

_____

_____

_____

_____

_____

_____

_____

_____

(continue on another sheet of paper)

When you finish writing, reread your essay. Does it flow smoothly from one paragraph to another? Do any sentences need rearranging? Could any of the main ideas use more details?

See if you can improve the first draft. Then write a final draft.

Essay — Final Draft

_____

_____

_____

_____

_____

_____

_____

_____

(continue on another sheet of paper)

The Spice Of Life

THINK

An outline for a story can be just a list of ideas put in the right order. Once you have your outline, you can develop several different stories by changing details. Here is a very basic outline for a story. It needs plenty of details. Fill in your own details for a short story.

I. The bedroom, that night

II. Can't get to sleep

III. The odd dream

IV. The next morning

WRITE

When you have finished the outline, write a short story that follows the same sequence of ideas. Be sure to start each paragraph in your story with a topic sentence, add descriptive words, and create interesting sentence patterns.

Short Story #1

_____

_____

_____

(continue on another sheet of paper)

Now, use this clean copy of the original outline to put in completely different details. Then write a second short story. The sequence of ideas should be the same, but the second story will sound much different.

I. The bedroom, that night

II. Can't get to sleep

III. The odd dream

IV. The next morning

Short Story #2

_____

_____

_____

(continue on another sheet of paper)

Name _____

A Day
In My Life

THINK

Think about an ordinary day in your life. The events follow a time sequence. Most of the things that happen in an ordinary day may not be exciting. But you can make the events more interesting by using vivid descriptions and a variety of word sequences.

Make a few notes about the things you do in a normal day. Then number the events in the order they happen.

Now, think about all the events. Brainstorm until you find something interesting about each. Don't make up events. Look at the ordinary ones in a new way. Discover the details that will make your day interesting to someone.

WRITE

Write about your day in a way that a reader will find interesting. Keep the events in order, starting with the beginning of your day. Include clear, colorful descriptions of all the events. End with the last event of the day.

_____

_____

_____

_____

_____

_____

(continue on another sheet of paper)

A Life Of Crime

THINK

Egbert is a criminal, and you are going to write a short biography about him. The questions below can help you organize your thoughts about Egbert. Some of the questions are followed by a few possible answers, but you should try to think of your own ideas.

What kind of criminal is Egbert? (jewel thief, computer thief, shoplifter)

Does he break the law often?

Why does he commit crimes? (fun, thrill, money)

Has he been caught?

Where is he now? (jail, hiding, Caribbean resort)

What is he doing?

List any other information you think might be important in Egbert's biography. You might want to include how he got started in crime, his childhood, how he got caught, or his future plans.

Once you've thought about Egbert's life, it's time to put your thoughts in order. Start at the beginning. Write down the earliest event you are going to cover, and then put the later events in order. Decide which events belong in the first paragraph. Then write down the main idea of that paragraph. Do the same for the other paragraphs (list the events and the main idea). You only need three or four paragraphs.

Once you decide on the main ideas, you may want to add more details, drop some, or rewrite your main ideas to fit the details you want to include.

WRITE

You are ready to write Egbert's biography. You already have a sequence for the story, but check each paragraph to make sure that the sequence is clear. Include some phrases that use the words "when," "as soon as," "until," "before," and "since." These phrases will help move the story along and make your sequence clear to your readers.

I'LL NEVER BE TAKEN ALIVE!
The Short Life of Egbert P. Slocum

By _____

_____

_____

(continue on another sheet of paper)

APPLES, ORANGES, AND "VROOTFRUITS"

Teacher's Guidelines:

Observing/Comparing/Classifying/Imagining

The activities in this unit emphasize four thinking skills: observation, comparison, classification, and imagination. These skills are closely related to each other and are often difficult to handle in isolation from one another.

Observation involves noticing and recording the facts, things, and events we see. As we observe, we automatically use comparison to note how each item relates to others in our experience. Comparisons help in classifying the item — i.e., putting it into an arrangement according to some systematic division by type. Each type, or class, includes and is limited to items having characterisitics in common. Finally, we can use the information that we observed, compared, and classified as the basis for forming mental images of what is not actually present or has never been experienced: in other words, imagining.

Observing

Careful observation, of course, is an important thinking and writing skill. "I Spy" and "Five Minutes" are the **THINK & WRITE** activities that emphasize observation and recording of aspects of daily life. In "I Thought I Saw A Pussycat," "Guess Who," and "Oh, What A Beautiful Morning," students are called upon to observe and describe animals, people, and the weather. As students become better observers, you can challenge them by requiring more detailed descriptions as well as descriptions of more complicated situations.

Comparing

We often compare one thing to another unconsciously, but in writing it is important to make this process a conscious one. The good writer, for example, compares various words and determines nuances of meaning before selecting the right one to use.

In "Meow, Purr, Meow," "Careful! Words Have Feelings, Too," and "Mosey, Stride, And Scamper," students compare synonyms in order to detect variations in meaning. Examining wants as opposed to needs is the basis of "But I Want To!" while "Driver Is To Car As . . . " introduces students to analogies, a form of comparison that involves making logical relationships. "Roar Like A Lion," "Fred's Head Went Dead," "He's So Small," and "I'd Rather Die Than . . . " carry practice in writing description a step further by presenting various types of figurative language as forms of comparison.

Comparison activities can also include comparing historical periods, geographic locations, and new vocabulary (in any subject). Even a bit of comparison shopping can help students recognize the importance of this thinking skill.

Classification

The third thinking skill in this unit is classification, including the development and use of classifying criteria. Two activities — "Capering Colors" and "Groups Big And Small" — deal with classifying by given systems. In "Where Should I Go?" students not only classify items but also develop their own categories. To expand the skills introduced in these activities, you can have your students experiment with known classification systems (science topics, musical categories, and literary forms work well) and then develop their own systems.

Imagining

The final section in this unit asks students to use thinking skills already presented in order to create new realities. Imaginative writing must be as clear as possible so that the reader will see the image just as the creator of the image sees it. The **THINK & WRITE** imagining activities begin with students creating imaginary individuals ("How Real Is Real?"), places ("Somewhere Over The Rainbow"), animals ("A Barlatom Followed Me Home"), a fairy tale ("Slimy Sid And Santa"), and aliens ("Meet Extet"). The last two activities — "Long Ago, In A Castle On A Hill" and "Let's Meet For Lunch On Mars" — require that students envision and describe whole cultures.

Many of the THINK sections of these activities can be used as group activities. Students need to see how others observe, compare, and classify. They must be exposed to different methods and possibilities; they must refine their own thoughts by defending their choices; and, finally, they must try to present their own imaginative efforts to an audience.

The following activities are just a starting point. Students will have to work at honing these skills until they can observe, compare, classify, and imagine effectively. Once they attain such mastery, their writing will display a greater clarity, more accurate description, and more frequent and appropriate use of figurative language.

I Spy

THINK

    How many times have you answered the question "What did you do today?" with "Oh, nothing."? But it's never really true. You are always doing something. People answer that way because they take most events in a normal day for granted.

    Think about your day today. What have you done so far? You have done things, even if they haven't been exciting or memorable. They are the little things, the daily routines, that make up life. If you think carefully, you can describe all the things that you've done since you woke up this morning.

    This sort of careful description of little things is called an "observation." Observing means to look closely at things. A good observer writes down all the details so that nothing is forgotten. And a good observer chooses his or her words with great care so that the description is accurate and complete. Some people write down their observations, along with their feelings and wishes, in a diary. It is very important, though, to keep feelings separate from observations.

WRITE

You are going to write a one-day diary observation about yesterday. Although the listing below is broken down into hours, you can divide it up even more if you want. Include everything you can recall about yesterday: where you were, what happened, and people you were with.

Describe everything as if you were an observer, watching what happened rather than really being a part of the day's events. Be sure to include plenty of details in order to make your observation interesting.

My Diary For _____ , 19 ____

8:00

9:00

10:00

11:00

12:00

1:00

2:00

3:00

4:00

5:00

6:00

7:00

8:00

9:00

Five Minutes

THINK

When you observe something, you watch it and write down what you see. Often, you don't have time to think much about what is going on while you are observing. You just make notes that you can use later to describe what you saw. You use words or phrases for your notes. You don't worry about writing complete sentences until later. You try to be like a camera, taking shot after shot of what is going on. When you're done observing, you should have a bunch of detailed word-pictures (your notes). Then you can write your description.

WRITE

Try doing five one-minute observations of five different things at five different times. Start by closing your eyes. When you open them, quickly pick something to observe. Write down what you see. If you get stuck, pick something else and keep writing.

Observation #1:

Observation #2:

Observation #3:

Observation #4:

Observation #5:

I Thought I Saw A Pussycat

THINK

Scientists observe animals. They try to describe everything they can about how the animals live. They describe the animals' actions, appearance, habits, and food. A scientific description has to be clear. It must tell exactly what the scientists observed and not include any personal opinions about the animal.

A scientist would say:

The cat curled up on a pillow in the sun.

A scientist would NOT say:

The cat looked so cute all curled up.

Saying that the cat looked cute is an opinion. It does not belong in a scientific observation.

WRITE

Observe any animal that will let you stay around it for awhile. Note what the animal looks like, how it acts, and some of its habits. Then write a short report about your observations. Try not to let your feelings about the animal creep into your description. Tell only what anyone would have seen watching the animal as you did.

_____

_____

_____

_____

_____

_____

_____

(continue on another sheet of paper)

Guess Who

THINK

Observing is watching and recording (writing down) what you see. It does *not* include an opinion of what you see. It *does* include plenty of details about what you see.

Three of the sentences below are observations. The other two sentences contain opinions. Circle the three sentences that are observations and could help you identify which girl was being watched.

She has brown hair and blue eyes.

She is a nice girl.

She sits up straight.

She wrinkles her forehead when she is thinking.

She never has any fun.

The second and fifth sentences give opinions, not observations. "Nice" tells how the writer feels about the girl. "Never has any fun" is also an opinion. What is fun to one observer may not be fun to another — or to the girl.

WRITE

Your teacher made up two lists with the names of everyone in your class, then cut the lists apart and put the names into a hat or bowl. Your whole class is going to play a guessing game.

Pick out two names. If you pick your own name, put it back and try again. If you get the same person's name twice, put one back and pick another.

Then, during the rest of the day, secretly observe the two classmates whose names you drew. Describe exactly what you see. Include plenty of details but *no* opinions. Try to describe each person so well that everyone in class will know who you were watching just by what you say about them.

Your teacher will put together a list of everyone's observations without saying who was being observed by whom. It's up to you to guess each person's identity from the list of observations.

Guess Who

Observations Of Classmate #1

Observations Of Classmate #2

Oh, What A Beautiful Morning

THINK

Snoopy, the beagle in the cartoon strip "Peanuts," has been writing a novel for many years. It always starts: "It was a dark and stormy night . . ." Snoopy is starting his story by setting the scene. He has included three words that tell us what it is like there when the story opens: dark, stormy, and night.

Writers often describe the weather to set a scene. Good writers do more than just tell what the sky looks like. They try to make a reader use all his or her senses. They tell what the air feels like: the temperature, wind, and wetness. They tell what the air smells like. They describe the sounds that can be heard. These writers want the reader to see, hear, feel, and smell the scene.

Note how the following paragraph appeals to your senses:

> The hedgehog stuck his head out of the hole. The bright sunlight made him blink and then sneeze. The warm, damp grass bowed in a slight breeze. The sun quickly baked winter's chill from his bones. Everything seemed bright and clean. Spring was in the air.

This paragraph sets the scene for a story by telling you about the weather. It tries to make you feel that you are there with the hedgehog on a bright spring morning.

A good weatherman wouldn't describe the same morning that way. He would describe it something like this:

> It was mostly sunny, with a few high clouds. Bright sun dried the dew. A slight breeze, 0-5 miles an hour, blew until noon. The temperature was in the 70s.

When you are writing, you must decide whether you are observing in order to set a scene or to give a scientific report. If you are a storyteller and want your readers to feel the weather with all their senses, then you must choose different words from those a weatherman would use.

WRITE

Pretend that you are a weatherman for a local TV station. Write a weather report for four separate days, one day for each season. Write one report for winter, one for spring, one for summer, and one for fall. Choose different kinds of weather (stormy, clear, windy, rainy, and so forth) for each day.

Tell your listeners exactly how cold, hot, stormy, etc., it is. Compare the day to another day so that they will understand. You might mention special clothes or rainwear your listeners will need. Make sure each description leaves no doubt as to what the weather is that day.

A Winter Day:

A Spring Day:

A Summer Day:

A Fall Day:

Now choose one of your reports and turn it into the opening paragraph of a short story. Use the same information, but change the weatherman's report into a storyteller's setting of the scene.

_____

_____

_____

_____

_____

_____

_____

_____

_____

(continue on another sheet of paper)

Meeow

Purrrr

Meow, Purr, Meow

THINK

Words that have almost the same meaning are called synonyms. Often, you can replace a word with its synonym in a sentence. Synonyms, however, don't always mean *exactly* the same thing. Look at the following sentences. See how the replacement of words with their synonyms changes the meaning. As a result, each sentence creates a little different picture in your mind.

> The man walked around the garden.
> The fellow strolled in the yard.
> The guy wandered through the flower beds.

We must know exactly what each word means in order to tell synonyms apart. A word's definition tells what makes that word slightly different from its synonyms. For example, read this sentence:

> The cat would _____ at the window when it wanted to
> come in.

We could fill in the blank with either "meow" or "purr." But if we know the definitions of these words, we can pick the right one for the meaning of the sentence.

Meow — A sound made by cats, usually with their mouths open. Often used to express needs (food, water, affection).

Purr — A low humming sound made by cats, especially when pleased. Comes from the back of the throat.

You should find it easy now to pick the right synonym to fill in the blank.

WRITE

Here are several pairs of sentences. The sentences in each pair are the same except for one word. Look up the definitions of each word. Write the definition that clearly tells how the word is different from its synonym. Write only the definition that applies to the sentence.

The man stopped to nap.
The man stopped to rest.
> nap:
>
> rest:

The girls giggled during the movie.
The girls laughed during the movie.
> giggled:
>
> laughed:

The lion chased the deer.
The lion hunted the deer.
> chased:
>
> hunted:

The sailor's tale was very funny.
The sailor's account was very funny.
> tale:
>
> account:

Careful!
Words
Have Feelings,
Too

THINK

Read the following sentences. Then decide which one describes the best party:

The party was fun.   The party was amusing.
The party was good.   The party was enjoyable.
The party was great.   The party was delightful.
The party was fine.   The party was pleasant.

Some words carry a meaning that has feelings attached to it. When we are writing, we need to think about the emotions that a word might make a reader feel. The emotions must fit the situation. If you want people to like or dislike something very much, you can choose words that will make your readers feel those emotions. But you must be careful in choosing your words. Even close synonyms can bring out much different emotions in a reader.

WRITE

Your best friend has had an accident and is in the hospital. Your father is away on a business trip. Write a short letter to each of them about the fieldtrip you just took with your class. Describe the same place and the same events in both letters. But write each letter so that it shows a different mood. One might sound excited and the other bored. Or one might be serious and the other silly. Choose your words carefully so that the person who receives your letter will feel the emotions you want him or her to experience.

Letter #1

Dear _____ ,

_____

_____

_____

_____

_____

_____

_____

(continue on another sheet of paper)

Letter #2

Dear _____ ,

_____

_____

_____

_____

_____

_____

_____

(continue on another sheet of paper)

Mosey, Stride, And Scamper

THINK

Some everyday words don't tell us as much as we'd like to know. These words are too general to give us a clear idea about a person or action. For example, consider the word "walk." Now think about all the synonyms for "walk" that provide a slightly different, often more interesting meaning.

> As the cowboy moseyed over to the girl, the fat man strode quickly away.

"Mosey" describes slow movements, while "stride" indicates long steps. A mouse would not stride, but it might scamper. These three words — mosey, stride, and scamper — give us a better sense of the way someone moves than the everyday word "walk" does.

Use your imagination, a thesaurus, and other books to find at least three synonyms for the words below.

want: _____

pain: _____

run: _____

power: _____

look: _____

pretty: _____

WRITE

Pick two words from each set of synonyms. When you're sure you know the differences in their meanings, write a sentence for each word. Your sentences should show some of the differences in meaning between the two synonyms.

_____

_____

_____

_____

(continue on another sheet of paper)

But
I Want
To!

THINK

Have you ever wanted something (really wanted it!) but didn't need it at all? People often compare what they want with what they need. A comparison of wants and needs — and of their reasons for the wants and needs — can help them decide what they should do.

You may find that making a list of wants and needs can help you make important decisions. For example, pretend that your family is looking for a new house to buy. You are helping by listing all the things your family needs in a new house (number of bedrooms, yard, family room, eat-in kitchen, etc.) and the things you would really like (large bedroom of your own, yard, etc.). See how your two lists compare.

Family Needs   **Your Wants**

WRITE

Today is very important because you have to make a final decision about something. Write a short story about your decision. Start by listing the needs and wants that must go into making your choice. In your story, be sure to include what choice you finally make and how you think that choice will turn out in the future.

Make up a situation if you don't have a real decision to make. It can be about almost anything. But you have to tell about how your wants and needs helped you decide.

Needs   **Wants**

One Tough Choice

_____

_____

_____

(continue on another sheet of paper)

Driver Is To Car As . . .

THINK

An analogy involves a comparison between different things. The comparison is based on some relationship between the things. Here is an analogy:

Driver is to car as farmer is to tractor.

Sometimes you find an analogy in which the end is left blank. You have to figure out the comparison and fill in the missing part. Try this analogy:

Driver is to car as pilot is to _____.

That was easy because the first analogy showed you how the things being compared were related. The driver controls a car the same way a farmer controls a tractor. In the second example, the driver controls a car the same way a pilot controls an airplane. "Airplane" is the word that goes in the blank to complete the analogy.

Not all analogies, however, use the same kind of comparisons. Try the ones below. Each one involves a different kind of comparison. Be sure you understand why you choose each word to complete the analogies.

1. Petal is to flower as feather is to _____ .

2. Artist is to picture as poet is to _____ .

3. Summer is to fall as spring is to _____ .

4. Mother is to father as aunt is to _____ .

5. Up is to down as in is to _____ .

Which analogy involved a comparison of opposites? _____ Of a specific order of time? _____ Of a person and product? _____ Of a part and its whole? _____ Of a family relationship? _____

WRITE

Now it is your turn to fill in the second half of analogies. Figure out how the things in each analogy are related, and then complete the comparison. Often, there is more than one right answer.

Left is to right as _____

    Compares:

Door is to house as _____

    Compares:

Fire is to smoke as _____

    Compares:

June is to August as _____

    Compares:

Corn is to grow as _____

    Compares:

Look at the ways to compare things listed below. Write an analogy for each way, but leave out the last word in each analogy. Then swap papers with a classmate. See if you can figure out each other's analogies.

1. Compare a whole and one of its parts.

2. Compare an action and the thing that does it.

3. Compare opposites.

4. Compare an object and how it is used.

Roar Like A Lion

THINK

Sometimes, in order to describe an object or person, we compare it to something completely different. We are not trying to say the two things are really alike. We are trying to create a lively picture of the thing or person we're describing.

Look at this sentence:

Dad roared like a lion.

Do see a picture like this in your mind?

Probably not. You understand the sentence to mean that Dad was yelling loudly, perhaps even ferociously.

This sort of comparison — between Dad and a lion — is an example of what is called *figurative language.* The writer who uses figurative language doesn't expect readers to believe that the two things in the comparison are exactly the same. The writer is using figurative language to create a lively description.

Look at these comparisons:

Mary was as quiet as a mouse.
The music was as soft as a whisper.
The mountains protected the valley like a fence.
The icy sidewalk was like glass.

Now that you have the idea, create a figurative-language comparison for each of the following sentences. There are many right answers, but you should be able to explain why your choice makes sense.

The dress was as _____ .
Monday was like _____ .
Fred snored _____ .
The tree swayed _____ .

WRITE

Your class took a trip to the zoo. Now your teacher wants you to write about the animals you saw there. Write a few sentences about each animal listed on the map below. Include one figurative-language comparison in each animal description. The comparison can describe how the animal looked or acted, or it can deal with some fact you know about the animal. Here's an example:

The bear slept like a log the whole time we were there.

_____

_____

_____

_____

_____

_____

_____

_____

(continue on another sheet of paper)

Fred's Head
Went Dead

THINK

Careful readers must know the difference between comparisons that are meant to be taken literally and comparisons that use figurative language.

The girl had the longest hair in the class (literal comparison).

The girl had coal black eyes (figurative-language comparison).

Sometimes, comparisons that use figurative language can be confusing. If you take the writer's words literally, you will get a silly picture. Look at the sentences below. Draw a little cartoon to show the literal meaning of each sentence.

His teacher tore his story apart.
She threw away her money.
When he got up to give his speech, Fred's head went dead.

Each of these sentences wants you to understand an idea: that the teacher found many things wrong with the story; that the girl wasted her money; and that Fred forgot what he wanted to say.

WRITE

Now it's your turn to create some comparisons, both literal and figurative. Imagine that you are sitting on a bench in the park. Describe some of the unusual, interesting, or beautiful things that you see. Remember, you show how you feel about things by the comparisons you choose to describe them.

_____

_____

_____

_____

_____

_____

(continue on another sheet of paper)

He's So Small

THINK

We often compare people to other people to help describe them.

> Bill's so small that he looks like a first grader.
> Jim is the tallest person in class. He is even taller than Mr. North.
> Mary has longer hair than anyone else in school.

Sometimes, we compare people to animals or objects. We don't mean these comparisons to be understood word for word. We want to express an idea in a lively way, not to make an exact comparison. That is one use of figurative language.

> Janet has legs like a stork.
> Mark is a walking encyclopedia.
> Nancy is as skinny as a lamppost.

A good description must include details as well as comparisons. Look at the following description. It contains interesting details along with comparisons to people, animals, and objects. It creates a picture in your mind about how this girl looks.

> Annette was the class shrimp. She was, however, as graceful as a swan. She had a small oval face, and her midnight black hair curled around it like a picture frame. Her eyes glittered like emeralds.

WRITE

You can use comparisons to write descriptions of people. Pick two different people, one a movie (or TV) star and the other a member of your family. Use both facts and comparisons to describe them. You can compare each one to animals, other people, or the whole world. Use some literal and some figurative-language comparisons.

_____

_____

_____

(continue on another sheet of paper)

Name _____

I'd Rather Die Than . . .

THINK

Every day we stretch the truth to create lively descriptions. "Big as a house," "tall as a tree" describe size through exaggeration. These comparisons are meant to make a point, not to say that one thing is actually as big as a house or as tall as a tree. You can use exaggeration to compare things in an interesting way. But if you use it too often, it loses its effect.

Think about walking down the street and seeing a big dog with long, skinny legs. How would you describe the dog's legs to a friend? Could you use exaggeration to make the point?

He had legs like a giraffe.
That was one dog with toothpicks for legs.
I never knew that a dog could walk on stilts.

WRITE

Write a sentence or two for each situation below. Use exaggeration to describe something or to make a point.

1. Your mother is forcing you to go to a family dinner party. You don't want to go, AT ALL! What do you tell her the party will be like for you?

_____

_____

The day after the party, how do you describe it to a friend?

_____

_____

2. You go to the zoo and spot a big, furry animal you'd love to have for a pet. Use exaggeration to describe it.

_____

_____

3. You are being punished. You cannot play in — or even go to — your team's championship game. What do you say to your parents about the way they are treating you?

_____

_____

Capering Colors

Crayons

THINK

Get the biggest box of colored pencils, crayons, markers, or paints that you can find. The more colors the better. You're going to group the colors. You must decide which category listed below to use for each color. The only rules are that you must put each color in just ONE category and that EVERY category must have at least one color in it.

Put a circle of color under the category you choose for that color. Before you start making circles, though, you might want to plan ahead so that each category has at least one color and that no color appears more than once.

Categories

Light Colors   Dark Colors

Warm Colors   Cool Colors

Colors You Like   Colors You Hate

WRITE

Now pretend that you have a new pot of white paint. You're going to add several colors, one at a time. Write a few sentences to tell how the paint changes with each color you add. Be sure to use vivid words to describe the colors and the amounts that you mix in. And be sure to keep the sequence clear.

_____

_____

_____

_____

_____

(continue on another sheet of paper)

Where Should I Go?

THINK

We often put things into groups without thinking much about them. We look at an item — a book, a car, or a dog — and we put the item into a group as soon as we say what it is. All the things in a particular group are alike in some ways. Those likenesses are what we use to classify the items. To classify means to put similar things into a group. Here are some items for you to classify.

jeans	bread	saw	cereal
shirt	cheese	pipe	ice cream
screws	butter	hammer	tie

Group the items below under the name of the place you are sure to find them.

Grocery Store   **Hardware Store**   **Clothing Store**

Now group the same items according to what they are made of.

Wood and Metal   **Grains**   **Milk**   **Cloth**

Finally, group the same items according to where a store gets them.

A Factory   **A Farm**

71

WRITE

You know how to put the same items into several different groups. Pick a topic that interests you, and list as many things as you can think of that are part of that subject. For instance, if your subject is cars, you can list different types of cars or the different parts of one car. For food, you can list different fruits, vegetables, meats, and so forth, or you can list the ingredients used to make certain dishes. List at least twelve different things for your topic.

Topic:

Items:

Look at your list carefully. Group some of the things together. You can group items by where they are found, what they are made of, their use, or anything else they have in common. Decide what makes this group go together, and give this group a name. Write the name at the top of the group of similar items.

Look at the items that are left in your first list. Group some of them under a different title. Be careful, though. You must not take items out of your first group to put into your second group. The groups must not overlap. Keep going until every item from your list fits into one — and only one — group.

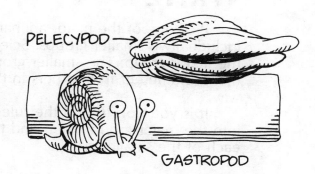

Groups Big And Small

THINK

Scientists group many things. They begin with big groups, and they divide each big group into smaller groups. Then they divide each smaller group into even smaller groups. Scientists group all animals and plants this way.

For example, scientists have put certain animals into one major group called "Mollusks." This major group contains two smaller groups: "Gastropods" and "Pelecypods." The names of these groups don't tell us much, though. We need to know what the rules are for putting certain animals in each group. A few examples would help us understand these groupings, too.

Mollusks — Animals with soft, boneless bodies. Most of them have shells.

Gastropods — Mollusks which have one-piece spiral shells or no shells. This group includes snails, slugs, and limpets.

Pelecypods — Mollusks which have two shells or a shell that opens and closes. This group includes mussels, oysters, and scallops.

You can add animals to these groups because now you know how the animals in each group are alike. Into which group would a sea snail go? A clam? Would a shark go into any of these groups?

WRITE

Pick one of the major animal groups below. Each major group includes two smaller groups. Scientists use the smaller groups to divide the major group. The smaller groups allow scientists to classify animals that are different from others in the major group in some important way.

It is your job to find the rule scientists use for putting an animal into the major group. Then find the rules for dividing the animals into each of the smaller groups.

Amphibians

Salientia

Caudata

Reptiles

Sauria

Chelonia

Birds

Falconiformes

Psittaciformes

Mammals

Monotremata

Primates

How Real Is Real?

THINK

Can you describe someone you've never met? Of course you can. Most people can describe Abraham Lincoln because they have read what Lincoln looked like, how tall he was, and so forth.

We can get to know many real and imaginary people through a writer's description. If the description is good, the person comes alive in our mind. We feel as though we actually know the character.

Often, when writers want to describe an imaginary person, they think about a real person. In some cases, they think about several real people and then put parts of the different real people together to create the imaginary character.

Think about six people you know. Think of how they look and act. Now pick one feature from each of the six, and list these features in the space below. You might pick the hair from one and the eyes from another. You might pick how one acts at school and how another walks. Just make sure that you have six features, one from each real person.

Think about what kind of person could have *all* the features you've listed. What features can you add to the description. Remember, you want your imaginary character to seem real but much different from anyone you know.

Character Features

WRITE

Use your notes to write a clear description of your character. No one else can see what you have created in your mind until you describe the person. You must describe your character so well that a reader will see the person in his or her mind just the way you do in your mind. Remember, this is an imaginary person. It may be based on real people, but it should not resemble any one person you know.

_____

_____

(continue on another sheet of paper)

Somewhere
Over
The Rainbow

THINK

Can you describe how a place looks, even if you have never been there? Of course you can. Some people have never seen a beach, but they can describe one. They have a picture in their mind. That picture is based on something they have read or a photograph they have seen. All they do is describe that picture.

When you describe a place — real or imaginary — you describe what you see in your "mind's eye." If you write a good description, then others will see almost the same picture in their mind's eye. How do you write a good description of a place? You start by carefully choosing words that will create a clear, vivid picture. These words should describe location, size, shape, and color.

WRITE

Here is a list of imaginary places. Pick three of them, and picture each one in your mind's eye. Then write a paragraph describing each one of the three places. Create a clear picture, first in your mind and then on paper. Try to include everything in your description that another person would need to know in order to see the places exactly as you do.

Prairie City   Fuller Farm   Zimms Street   Sewer Swamp
The Measley's Mansion   Hootville   The Princely Palace
Park Place   The Wish Shop   Simpson Park

_____

_____

_____

_____

_____

_____

(continue on another sheet of paper)

A Barlatom Followed Me Home

THINK

A barlatom is an imaginary animal. It is a mean little creature, with a small roundish body and a long fuzzy tail. It is about the size of a fat woodchuck or raccoon, but it has six short legs with eagle-like talons at the end of each leg. On top of the goose-like neck is a small pointy head, and long hair hangs down from its head like a beard.

The barlatom's mouth is filled with sharp teeth, and it has beady little eyes. Its grey fur is long and shaggy, like a sheepdog's. Because of its long hair, short legs, and fat belly, the barlatom can't run very fast.

Now it's your turn to create an imaginary animal. First, list the things you want to tell about your animal. Include a description of his color, his body parts, and perhaps even how he acts. In order for others to imagine him as you do, you must write clear descriptions. One of the most effective ways to describe your creature is to compare and contrast it with animals most people already know about. Look back at the descriptions of the barlatom's size, talons, neck, and fur.

When you finish your list, group similar parts together. Grouping similar parts together will help your description flow smoothly.

WRITE

Write a paragraph or two describing your imaginary creature. Don't forget to name him. Then ask a friend to draw a picture of your animal based on your description. DON'T WATCH AND DON'T OFFER ANY HELP OR ADVICE! If the drawing doesn't seem right to you, rethink your description and rework some of your comparisons. Then ask someone else to try drawing the animal.

_____

_____

_____

_____

_____

(continue on another sheet of paper)

Slimy Sid
And Santa

THINK

Everyone has read fairy tales and folk tales. Most of these stories are very old, and the characters have been familiar to many generations of children.

But that's no reason why you can't invent a new fairy tale or folk character. Start by selecting one of your favorite figures from fairy or folk tales like the Pied Piper, Santa Claus, Cinderella, Robin Hood, Casey Jones, Little Red Riding Hood, Snow White, John Henry, or any other one you know. Think about this character until you have a clear picture of him or her in your mind.

Now create your own fairy tale or folk character. You can create a hero (usually handsome), a heroine (usually beautiful), or a villain (almost always ugly). Be sure you know what makes your character special — bravery, beauty, evilness, etc. Think about your new character until you can see him or her clearly in your mind.

WRITE

Plan a story in which the two characters — your favorite from fairy or folk tales and your new creation — meet. Start by making notes about where, how, and why they meet and what happens when they get together. Then write a short story based on your notes. Be sure to describe both of the characters as well as the place and the action. Use your imagination to make your characters interesting and your story exciting.

_____

_____

_____

_____

_____

(continue on another sheet of paper)

Meet Extet

THINK

Think of all the different creatures from outer space that you have seen on TV or in the movies. Each alien is different. Some aliens look very strange, and some look almost human. Each one began as an idea in a writer's mind. Then the writer had to describe the idea to an artist. The artist drew pictures based on the description. Finally, the artist's drawings served as a guide to people who make models or who design the makeup for the actors.

When a writer starts creating an alien, he or she must think about several things. The writer has to think about size, shape, color, and how the alien communicates. He or she must decide if the alien will look scary or friendly. Very often, the writer begins by comparing the alien to a person, then decides how much the alien should look like a human.

WRITE

You work in Hollywood as a writer for one of the big movie studios. The studio is planning to make a new movie about aliens from outer space. The producer has three stories and can't decide which one to make into the movie. He wants you to describe your ideas for these aliens. A drawing would help, but it isn't necessary.

Read the three storylines on the next page. Create a different alien for each one. Write a clear, interesting description of each. Don't describe aliens that you have seen in movies or on TV before. The studio can't use aliens that anyone has ever seen. These aliens must be different from any others.

Storyline #1: Alien spaceships come to Earth seeking food. Their planet has been destroyed, and they are very hungry. But they are friendly aliens.

Description:

Storyline #2: Spacemen from Earth crash on a dead-looking planet. They are threatened by cruel aliens who live under the ground.

Description:

Storyline #3: Farmers have moved to another planet to grow food for people back on Earth. They discover extremely smart aliens living in the forest. The farmers do not know at first whether the aliens are friendly or hostile.

Description:

Long Ago,
In A Castle
On A Hill

THINK

Many writers like to create stories that take place long ago in the distant past. To write such stories, they must learn what it was like to live back then. They study letters, books, and other materials written during that time. These writers try to find out what people thought, how they acted, and what they did. Sometimes writers even examine paintings, furniture, and clothing to help them understand how people of another era lived.

Writers of nonfiction try to stick to the facts when they write about the distant past. They are not interested in putting imaginary material into their writing.

Writers of historical fiction, though, use facts to help them make up imaginary people, places, and events. They often combine factual and imaginary material to create a story.

WRITE

Here are some facts about life in a medieval castle:

Castles had thick stone walls all around them. These walls went around a large yard and several buildings. The horses lived inside these walls along with the people of the castle. The main building, also made of stone, was usually very big and contained many rooms. Lots of servants were needed to help run the castle.

Most castles were damp and cold. The only heat came from the fireplaces. Each room had a fireplace. But some rooms were so big that the fireplace couldn't heat the whole area. Cooking was done in the kitchen fireplace. The kitchen was on the bottom floor, and the bedrooms were on the top.

If the children were rich, they had tutors to teach them. If the children were poor, they often received no education. Instead, they worked at special jobs in the kitchen, house, or barn.

Use these facts to write a story. Create a picture in your mind with the facts. Then invent some people who live in your medieval castle. Finally, make up an adventure. Tell where your characters go, what they see, and what they do. Have something exciting happen to them.

Show that you know your facts as you describe people, places, and events. If you don't know enough facts for your story, find out more about the Middle Ages. Be careful not to include anything modern (like bathrooms, heaters, running water, electricity) in your story.

Look at the topics listed below. They can help you organize your story. Make some notes for each topic and develop some ideas in your head before you begin writing.

Castle	Characters	Adventure
Size	Description	Where
Rooms	Jobs	When
People	Activities	People
Activities		Outcome

_____

_____

_____

_____

_____

_____

_____

(continue on another sheet of paper)

Let's Meet
For Lunch
On Mars

THINK

Think about the future. What will life be like in 100 years? We know that things have changed a lot in the last 100 years. What will happen in the next 100?

No one can really know, but we can make guesses. We must use our imagination to create the future. Think about the important things that are happening today. Think about the problems people are trying to solve and the new inventions people are working to develop. Let your mind imagine what life will be like 100 years from now when these problems are solved and people are using those inventions.

WRITE

Pick two of the following topics, and write a few paragraphs about each one. Tell about the future based on what is happening today. Invent machines, jobs, even new foods. Describe each item clearly. Remember, your reader has no idea what *you* think the future will be. You must describe your vision in detail.

To get started, answer the questions under your topics. Then use your imagination to come up with many more ideas about the future.

Transportation

How do people get from place to place?

How are things shipped to stores, homes, etc.

Jobs

What kinds of work do people do?

Are there factories, offices, schools, etc.

Does everyone work?

Homes

Where do people live?

Do they have houses or do they live in apartments?

Do they have plenty of room or is everyone crowded?

Leisure

How do people spend their time when they are not working?

What do they do for fun?

What are their hobbies?

Where do they go on vacations?

Food

What kinds of food do people eat?

Is their food natural or manmade?

Where does the food come from?

How is their food prepared?

Travel

Do people stay on Earth or do they travel into space?

Where do they go?

How do they get there?

What do they do once they get where they want to be?

_____

_____

_____

_____

_____

_____

_____

_____

_____

_____

_____

(continue on another sheet of paper)

NO PHONY BALONEY
Teacher's Guidelines: Evaluating

This unit emphasizes thinking and writing skills necessary to present facts, persuade others, and express emotions. It also aims (1) to heighten student awareness of writing that contains opinions, (2) to make them more sensitive to distinctions between facts and opinions, and (3) to recognize the differences between emotive and objective writing. Students are called upon to evaluate their own writing as well as other material for bias, emotions, opinions, facts, and logic.

Facts And Opinions

The first section, *Using Facts In Writing*, deals with finding, organizing, and using factual material successfully. In "Ready, Action," students determine main ideas and organize given facts. In "From *Family Circle* to *Sports Illustrated*," they must determine their audience, develop main ideas, and then write an outline for an article suitable for the specific audience. This activity also introduces the point that writers can use the same facts to write a variety of articles of interest to a number of different audiences.

The search for facts, the various ways to obtain them, and the organization of factual material in a way readers can understand provide the basis for several activities. "Where, Oh Where, Is My Little Black Book?" deals with the search for facts; "I'll Prove It" covers various types of searches; "Pillars And Posts" presents some main ideas and then requires students to obtain their own facts; and "Facts, Facts, And More Facts" shows how to use a survey to obtain facts.

As students search for facts, they will inevitably come up against opinions presented as facts. The second section of this unit, *Watching For Opinions*, is designed to help them spot such opinions and to make them aware of how generalized beliefs must be supported by facts in order to be convincing. "The Facts And Only The Facts" and "It's Right . . . And Wrong" are two actvities that emphasize these skills. "The World Is Flat And That's That" sensitizes students to particular words that can inject opinions into factual writing.

You can expand upon these **THINK & WRITE** activities by encouraging students to take a stand on current local, national, and international events and then having them express their ideas in articles, letters, and editorials. Their writing should display a clear recognition of what is fact and what is opinion, and every opinion should be well supported with appropriate facts.

Persuasive Writing

Students — along with the rest of us — confront persuasive writing daily. Many students readily recognize a piece of persuasive writing when they see one, but few have any experience in actually writing such a piece themselves. In "Please Come" and "Definitely The Greatest," students write informal persuasive letters to friends. "I Don't Agree" takes a more formal approach to the same skill, requiring a letter to the editor of the school newspaper. Political commentary and speeches are the focus of "Yesterday, In Washington," "Convince Me," and "I Give You The Next President Of The United States, Mr. Moo!" "New, Improved Crud" and "You'll Love This One" deal with print and radio advertising, respectively.

Emotive Vs. Objective Writing

The last section of this unit dwells on the differences between writing that appeals to the emotions and writing that tries to steer clear of any such appeal. "The House On The Corner" and "The Proper Time And Place" have students turn objective descriptions into emotional accounts, while "Dear Ann Landers:" and "Dear Sir:" are clear-cut examples of the enormous difference between an emotional letter and one that is strictly business. Reporting an event objectively as opposed to injecting emotion-laden personal details provides the basis for the final activities in the unit: "You Should Have Been There!" "A Reporter's Job," "Disaster," and "Thank Heaven."

Throughout this unit, students should constantly be evaluating their own writing to determine if they have expressed themselves clearly, supported their general statements with facts, and put their ideas in a way that their audience will find convincing. They should also be casting a more critical eye on other writing — textbooks, magazine articles, newspaper reports, even letters from friends — in order to hone their evaluating skills. The ability to examine all the nuances and hidden meanings in what they read as well as in what they write is a skill every student should develop.

Ready, Action

THINK

To write just about any kind of a report, you must first gather some facts. And that means doing research. Once you have the facts, you must organize them. You have to pick out the main topics and match each topic with supporting facts.

When you put the topics into a logical order, you create an outline for your report. Many writers change their outlines while they are actually preparing their reports. But that first outline is an important beginning to writing a well-organized report.

WRITE

Write a report about early radio based on the list of facts below. First, read the facts and decide which ones you want to be the main topics in your report. Then, organize the topics by numbering each one in the order you want it to appear.

After you number the topics, study the facts again. Group them with the topics they support. Finally, write a report that uses nearly all of the facts. Each paragraph in your report should begin with a topic sentence, and it should include the appropriate supporting facts.

Facts

The first radios had earphones.

Many of the early shows, like *Fibber McGee and Molly*, were comedies.

The whole family would listen to the radio together.

It was hard to tune in the station you wanted.

Everyone — rich and poor, old and young — listened to the radio.

In the early days of radio, most shows were local.

Among the most popular shows were adventure and mystery stories like *Superman* and *The Shadow*.

Often, listeners would pick up messages from ship and police radios.

"Soap operas" got their name because many of the shows were sponsored by companies that made soap.

Many people who came to the United States from other countries learned to speak English by listening to the radio.

On some nights, people listening to their radios would hear broadcasts from all over the world.

Main Topics:

Outline:

Report

_____

_____

_____

_____

_____

_____

_____

_____

(continue on another sheet of paper)

From
Family Circle
To
Sports Illustrated

THINK

Good writers can use the same set of facts to create many articles and stories. Often, they can sell their stories to several different magazines.

They can do this because every magazine wants articles aimed at its particular audience. The magazine tries to keep its audience interested by publishing articles it thinks its readers will like. Look at this list of magazine titles.

Pretty	*Craft Kraze*	*Auto Future*
Judo News	*Rockin' Muzik*	*Star Stories*
Kumpute	*Garden Perfect*	*Thrill Sports*

Each title tells you something about the magazine and its audience. Pick three of the titles above, and write a brief description of who you think might read each magazine. Then write a few words about the subjects the magazine probably covers.

_____

_____

_____

_____

_____

A magazine writer would look at the list of magazines and see several ways to use the same facts. For instance, *Auto Future* might want a story about the newest racing car; *Star Stories* could be interested in a report on a famous person who owns the newest racing car; and *Thrill Sports* would certainly want an article on how the newest racing car won its first competition.

WRITE

Pick two very different magazines from the list above. Now choose one topic that would interest the audiences of both magazines. List six facts for that topic.

Topic:

1.

2.

3.

4.

5.

6.

Plan an article for each magazine, using some of the same facts in both articles. Keep in mind that each article must interest the magazine's audience. Write the title and a brief outline for each article.

Name of Magazine 1:

    Article Title:

        Outline:

Name of Magazine 2:

    Article Title:

        Outline:

Where, Oh Where, Is My Little Black Book?

THINK

Everyone carries a little black book, filled with facts, inside his or her head. Besides the facts themselves, the little black book contains places and ways to get more facts. Write down all of the places and ways you think are in *your* little black book.

Places And Ways To Get Facts

Did you include interviewing people? Using an almanac? Calling the public library? Using the index in a textbook? Reading maps? There are thousands of different places and ways to find facts. Try to get more of them into your little black book!

WRITE

Here are fourteen questions. You can answer each question with a simple fact. Facts, though, are not always easy to find. You might have to look several places before you find the right fact. For these questions, use as many different sources as you can find. List both the answer and where you found it.

To make your search easier, underline key words in each question. Choose words that you might find in the title of an article that has the fact in it. A few key words are underlined for you.

1. What is the capital of <u>Florida</u>?

   Answer: Source:

2. What famous book did <u>Kenneth</u> <u>Grahame</u> write in 1908?

   Answer: Source:

3. Where do <u>wombats</u> live?

   Answer: Source:

4. What is a scale in music?

   Answer: Source:

5. Who starred in the 1944 movie "National Velvet"?

   Answer: Source:

6. What artist of the Italian Renaissance drew plans for a flying machine?

   Answer: Source:

7. What kind of shop did the Wright Brothers run while they worked on their first airplane?

   Answer: Source:

8. What is the longest river in the world?

   Answer: Source:

9. How old was Mozart when he died?

   Answer: Source:

10. Who are your state's senators?

    Answer: Source:

11. When was the first national TV program broadcast?

    Answer: Source:

12. What is the most dangerous nonpoisonous snake?

    Answer: Source:

13. What do coal and diamonds have in common?

    Answer: Source:

14. What is the real name of Dr. Seuss?

    Answer: Source:

I'll Prove It!

THINK

The world is filled with fact hunters, people who spend much of their time searching for facts. Doctors, lawyers, historians, and politicians all search for facts. Detectives, too, are well-known fact searchers.

Doctors search for the causes of sickness. They search books, magazines, and reports for facts. They do research to discover what causes people to get sick and how sick people can get well again.

Historians search through old letters, papers, books, and other objects of the past. They are searching for facts about what life was like, how famous events really happened, and why a particular person was special.

Think of other fact hunters. Think about the different kinds of facts they search for and how they find their facts.

WRITE

Create a story character who is a fact searcher of some sort. The search can be for facts about a murder, a disease, a famous person, or even an old car. The story you write should explain how the searcher finds the facts. Tell about the research, the clues, and the final discovery.

Before you start writing your story, plan your search by filling in the following outline. Use your imagination to make up clues, but be sure to place them in a logical order.

Character (name and description):

Searching For:

Research Steps:

1.

2.

3.

4.

5.

Major Clues:

1.

2.

3.

4.

5.

Final Discovery:

The Story Of A Search

_____

_____

_____

_____

_____

_____

_____

_____

(continue on another sheet of paper)

94

Pillars
And Posts

THINK

In most kinds of writing, if you want to make a general statement, you must support it with facts. For example, if you want to say "All sports are dangerous," then you must back up that statement with facts. You would probably point to football injuries, tennis elbow, hockey fights, and so forth to support your general statement.

Not everyone would agree with your general statement. Some people would present facts to support the opposite side. But if you want people to believe a general statement, you must support your statement with facts.

Here are several general statements about sports and exercise. Pick one of the statements, and then do research to find facts which support your choice.

Soccer is the up-and-coming sport in the United States.
Jogging can be dangerous.
Exercise can put you in a better mood.
The football field is a combat zone.
Car racing is a company sport.
Football is the most popular spectator sport.

Your statement:

Facts:

WRITE

Write a paragraph in which you support your general statement with the facts you found.

_____

_____

(continue on another sheet of paper)

Facts, Facts, And More Facts

THINK

One way to find facts about what people think is to conduct a survey. In a survey, you ask questions and record each person's answers. Then you put the answers together. The information you get from everyone's answers tells you something about people, what they do, what they like, and so forth.

You can take a survey to learn facts about your class. First choose a topic. Then write five specific questions. You can ask questions about things like family size, house size, birth dates, and favorite subjects, books, or shows. Ask everyone in class the same five questions. Write down each answer.

Hint: To make it easier to put the information together at the end of your survey, write questions that have either multiple-choice or very short answers.

Question 1:

Question 2:

Question 3:

Question 4:

Question 5:

WRITE

Now use the facts from your survey to write a report about your class. Make sure your report contains only facts and not opinions. For example, "Thirty students in class like the food in the cafeteria" is a factual statement. "The class thinks the cafeteria food stinks" is not a factual statement. You should be able to support every statement in your report with facts drawn from your survey.

_____

_____

_____

(continue on another sheet of paper)

The Facts
And
Only The Facts

THINK

A fact is something that has actually happened or is true. Sometimes facts get mixed up with opinions. An opinion is a belief. It seems true, but it is not always based on knowledge.

Opinions creep into factual writing all the time. Often they are easy to spot. Read these sentences about health. Cross out the sentences that express opinions.

A person needs to eat a variety of foods.
Beef is the best meat.
Fruits and vegetables contain important vitamins.
Milk and cheese are dairy products.
Peanut butter is great for lunch.
The "All Zucchini Diet" is wonderful.

Did you cross out the three sentences that contain opinions? Words like "best" and "wonderful" are clues. The second, fifth, and sixth sentences do not say, "I think . . . ," but you could add those words to the three sentences. They are opinion sentences. They tell what the writer believes, not what is fact.

WRITE

You are going to write a short newspaper article about your class. To get ready, make two lists. In one list put facts about your class. In the other list, write some opinions about your class. Be sure you put each fact and each opinion in its proper list.

Facts   **Opinions**

When you finish your lists, write the article. Put the facts into the first paragraph. Put the opinions into the second paragraph. Then write a three- or four-word headline that expresses your *opinion*. The headline will be the title of your article.

_____

_____

_____

(continue on another sheet of paper)

The World
Is Flat
And That's That

THINK

Sometimes, people get ideas stuck in their heads. They believe their ideas are facts, but they have no information to back up their beliefs. Often, they will not even accept facts that go against their opinions.

For example, many people did not believe Christopher Columbus when he tried to explain the facts that showed the world was round. They laughed at him. Their opinion was that the world was flat, and that was that!

Here is a report about Christopher Columbus that has facts mixed up with opinions. Your job is to take out the opinions by changing or dropping words and sentences. Sometimes, a whole sentence is an opinion. In other cases, you can drop just one or two words to change a sentence from an opinion to a fact. Be especially careful to find words that have hidden opinions. The underlined words and sentence are examples of what you should change or drop to make this a factual report.

CHRISTOPHER COLUMBUS

Christopher Columbus was the bravest sailor there ever was. He had a wonderful idea. He thought the Earth was round. He was sure that you could go east—to India—by sailing west.

Columbus asked many of the kings in Europe for money and ships. These <u>dumb</u> kings wouldn't listen to him. <u>The only smart ones were the King and Queen of Spain.</u> They listened to Columbus's <u>strange</u> plan. But they were too busy fighting the <u>evil</u> Moors and couldn't take time to help him.

Columbus kept <u>bothering</u> people. At last, Spain gave him some ships. The King and Queen promised him a big reward if he found India.

The crew was scared. These <u>cowards</u> wanted to turn back. They were sure they would fall off the end of the world. No one had ever sailed that far west. <u>They spent too much time praying they wouldn't die and not enough time having faith in Columbus's brains.</u> They had good weather as they crossed the Atlantic Ocean.

When the crew finally saw some birds, they got brave again. They sailed to some islands. Since Columbus thought these islands were near India, he named them the "Indies" and gave the people the <u>cute</u> name "Indians." Then he sailed around the <u>nice</u> islands for awhile before going back to Spain.

The King and Queen <u>sort of</u> rewarded him. Then they sent him back to the islands to be the governor of the area. Columbus did <u>terrible</u> things to the Indians. He forced them to change their religion. He made them bring him gold and jewels. He even sent Indians back to Europe as slaves.

Finally, the <u>foolish</u> King and Queen got mad at Columbus. They were greedy for more gold. He was a complete failure because he had not reached India. This <u>smart, brave</u> sailor died believing he had done nothing important.

WRITE

When you have taken out all of the opinions, rewrite the report on Columbus. Use the same facts, but be careful not to add opinions of your own. Use clear descriptions. Make sure none of your words contains hidden opinions.

CHRISTOPHER COLUMBUS

_____

_____

_____

_____

_____

_____

_____

_____

_____

_____

_____

_____

_____

_____

_____

_____

_____

_____

(continue on another sheet of paper)

It's Right...
And Wrong

THINK

You know that you use facts to support general statements. But did you know that you can put the same facts together in different ways to support opposite statements?

Here are two paragraphs about television. The paragraphs show how facts can support much different ideas about the same subject. Many of the facts are the same, but they support two very different general statements.

TV is a window on the world. Even the TV shows that are poorly written tell us something about the world. The best shows bring interesting people and places into our homes. Comedies tell us about people who live a different type of life from the one we live. Some shows take us to places we could never go in person. News programs often take us to danger zones. Through TV, we can visit the world without ever leaving our chair.

Most TV shows are worthless. The stories are poorly written. Children see and learn things on TV that they shouldn't be seeing and learning. Shows about places that people can't go to just make them unhappy with their lives. Because you see the world while you just sit in a chair, TV takes away your responsibility to make your life interesting.

WRITE

Pretend your town is having trouble deciding whether to build more playgrounds. Some people feel that playgrounds are too dangerous. Others believe that the town needs more playgrounds because children should play outside as much as possible.

Pick one of the following activities and do it. No matter which activity you choose, start with a general statement and then support it with facts. Be sure you include some of the same facts for both sides.

1. Write an announcement for a town meeting to be held this week. Describe the speaker who supports building more playgrounds and the speaker who is against building more playgrounds. Be sure to include each speaker's opinions.

2. Write a newspaper article that tells about the town meeting. Present both sides of the issue. Then give your own opinion as to which side you believe is right.

3. Write a letter to the editor of the local newspaper. Tell what position you take on the playground issue and why. Then write another letter to the editor taking the other side.

_____

_____

_____

_____

_____

_____

_____

_____

_____

_____

_____

_____

_____

_____

_____

(continue on another sheet of paper)

Please Come

THINK

You are giving a very special party, and you want a very special friend to come to it. You gather your courage and decide to write a persuasive invitation, so persuasive that you're sure the person will agree to come to your party.

First, make some notes about the party you plan to give. The party should be the absolute best event you can imagine, and your description should make it sound as terrific as you imagine it. Then, make some notes about your friend. Describe him or her, including likes and dislikes and reasons why he or she will have a great time at your party.

Party: _____

_____

_____

Friend: _____

_____

_____

WRITE

Using your notes, write an invitation that persuades — but does not beg — the person to come to your party.

Dear _____ ,

_____

_____

_____

_____

_____

(continue on another sheet of paper)

Definitely
The Greatest

THINK

Pretend that you have recently moved to a new town. You had to leave your best friend behind. Both of you hate being apart. You are just getting settled in your new home and school when you get a letter from your friend. He wants to know what it's like there because his parents are thinking about moving to the same town!

You are thrilled, but you know that you had better write a convincing letter. His parents want facts. List the things you like about your new town (it can be a real town or one you invent). Think of things his parents would consider important, as well as things your friend would like. List as many facts as possible to back up your opinion that your new town is "definitely the greatest."

Facts About Town

WRITE

Write a letter to your friend. Tell about the things to do in town, the schools, the stores, and what the place looks like. Try to convince your friend and his parents that it is a wonderful place to live. Don't be emotional. That won't sound convincing. Instead, use facts to back up all your general statements about what a great town it is.

Dear _____ ,

_____

_____

(continue on another sheet of paper)

I Don't Agree

THINK

Newspapers have a special place where they print "letters to the editor." People write letters to the editor to express their opinions and to try to persuade other readers. Sometimes, the letters are about an article that appeared in the paper. Other times, the letter writers want to bring problems to the attention of the paper and its readers.

Everybody can find something in school that should be changed. It might be the food, the amount of homework, the books, or the length of recess. Choose one thing you would like to see changed. Think about how you could convince the principal to change it. Develop good arguments, and try to find facts that support your arguments. List the important points that you need to cover. Then list the facts that support those points.

Change Needed:

Why Change Is Needed:

Supporting Facts:

WRITE

Pretend that you have a school newspaper. Write a letter to the editor about the problem you chose. Explain your opinion and the reasons for it. Use facts to support every general statement. Try to persuade everyone that you are right.

_____

_____

_____

(continue on another sheet of paper)

Yesterday, In Washington

THINK

Editorials express opinions. They are usually written by the people in charge of a newspaper or a radio or TV station. Good editorials use facts to support an opinion.

Think about some events that are happening around the world. Pick one current event. It can be a national, state, or local event — or even something happening in school. Study the facts by reading newspapers, listening to the news, and, if possible, talking to the people involved.

As you study the facts, form your own opinion. When you have enough facts, put your well-supported opinion into words. Tell the reasons why you have formed this opinion. BACK UP YOUR OPINION WITH FACTS!

Opinion: _____

_____

Supporting Facts: _____

_____

_____

WRITE

Once you feel sure of your opinion and the supporting facts, write a short editorial. Pretend you are presenting it on the radio or TV. Try to convince the people listening that you have a good argument. Do this by supporting each part of your argument with facts. Don't just make general statements.

_____

_____

_____

_____

(continue on another sheet of paper)

Name _____

Convince Me

THINK

When a candidate is running for office, he tries to convince the voters that he is the best person for the job. He does this by talking about ideas and programs and the things that should be changed. Often, the candidate makes every speech a little different so that his words are right for each audience.

Pretend that you are running for school president. You have to speak to every grade level. What would you include in your speeches? What kinds of changes would you suggest? What new ideas do you have? What programs would you like to start? List the items that you would put into your speeches in the space below.

Once you have listed these things, go back and put stars next to the ones that apply to the kindergarteners. You will have to put these items into words that five-year-olds can understand. You have to convince them that you are the best candidate for school president.

Now, go back over your list and check the items that you would include in a speech for fifth graders. Some items that have stars will also get check marks. But some of the things you would say to the kindergarteners won't interest the fifth graders. You will have to come up with a little different speech to convince the older group that you are the best.

WRITE

Write two speeches, one for the kindergarteners and one for the fifth graders. First, outline the important points for each speech. Then, when you have the points in a good order, fill in the facts to support each idea.

When you are pleased with your outlines, begin writing your speeches. When you finish, read them aloud. Often, something that looks right on paper doesn't sound right when read aloud. Make sure that each speech is aimed at the appropriate grade level. Remember that kindergarteners can't sit still as long as fifth graders can. In each case, you must convince your audience that you are the best candidate for school president.

Outline for Kindergarten Speech   *Outline for Fifth-Grade Speech*

Speech for Kindergarten

_____

_____

_____

(continue on another sheet of paper)

Speech for Fifth Grade

_____

_____

_____

(continue on another sheet of paper)

I Give You The Next President Of The United States, Mr. Moo!

THINK

When people run for office, they make many speeches. Most of these speeches have the same purpose: to persuade voters to vote for the candidate. The most convincing speeches combine general statements, opinions, facts, and even some emotion.

The candidate knows that the voters want facts. They want to know who he is and what his qualifications are for the office. They also want to know the candidate's opinions, and they expect the candidate to support his opinions with facts.

You are going to write a political speech. Pick an office to run for and decide on an audience who will hear your speech. Plan your speech carefully with this audience in mind. You would not present the same speech to the "Football Fans of America" as you would to the "Society of American College Professors." Decide what main ideas and opinions you will include. You want to cover the issues that are important to voters in general and the ones important to this audience in particular. Make sure you have supporting facts for every general statement and opinion.

As you write the speech, keep in mind that it must be well organized. If the speech is confusing, no one will understand it — much less be persuaded to vote for you. In addition, try to make the speech show what kind of a person you are. If you are a serious person, your speech should show it. If you like to tell jokes, you can include one or two in your speech.

WRITE

Candidate for: _____ (office)

Audience: _____

Main Ideas and Opinions

1.

2.

3.

4.

Supporting Facts

Use your outline to write the speech. Remember, organize the speech before you begin writing it. Read the speech aloud to make sure it sounds right. Often, what looks good on paper doesn't sound right when spoken. Finally, ask yourself if people will be persuaded to vote for you after they hear your speech. If not, is there anything you can change in your speech to make it more persuasive?

Vote for Me!

_____

_____

_____

(continue on another sheet of paper)

New, Improved Crud

THINK

Advertising is a special kind of writing. It tries to convince an audience to buy something. Look at some magazine ads, especially the big fancy ones. This is the kind of ad you are going to create.

Before you can create the ad, you must make some decisions:

1. What kind of product are you selling? _____

   What is its name (try something catchy)? _____

2. Who will buy the product (kids, housewives,

   executives, etc.)? _____

   Which magazines do these people read? _____

   _____

Now you have your product (#1) and your audience (#2). Think about the product and what is special about it. Then think about your audience and their interests. List some facts about the product and the audience below.

Product:

Audience:

WRITE

Pick one of your audience's interests. Draw a picture that will appeal to people with that interest. Now, write a sentence of five or six words that ties your product to the audience interest. Your sentence should be clever and catchy.

Then, write a few sentences that tell why your product is special and why your audience should use it. Finally, write a brief description of how you see the ad in your mind. Explain where the interest picture, product picture, headline sentence, and other words should be. The person who designs your ad for the magazine needs this information.

You'll Love
This One

THINK

Radio advertisements try to convince you, but they can't show you anything. They can't even use fancy art work to catch your attention.

You are going to write a radio ad for a place — a store, an amusement park, a vacation spot, or a museum. It is your job to make the place sound so interesting that people will want to go there. You do this by describing all the good things about the place and by making sure that every general statement has facts to support it.

You must decide, of course, what audience you want your ad to reach. If you are trying to reach kids, you will describe a place differently than if you are trying to reach older people.

Place:

Audience:

Main Points In Ad:

Facts Supporting Main Points:

WRITE

Write a 30-second radio ad that includes a description of the place and at least one general statement with facts to support it. You don't need to stick strictly to the facts, though. You can play on your audience's emotions, too. What would make your audience *really* want to visit this place? Be sure to include the answer to this question in your ad.

_____

_____

_____

_____

(continue on another sheet of paper)

Name _____

The House
On The Corner

THINK

You can describe the same thing many different ways. In fact, by choosing your words carefully, you can describe a very ordinary thing in a way that makes it sound unusual.

Picture a house, any house. You can describe it factually, or you can describe it in a way that makes others *feel* something about the house.

For example:

The large white house had a fence around it.

The huge house was peeling its dirty white paint. The fence was rotting, and the gate hung on one hinge.

The factual description of a house should include only what you can see: size, color, shape, number of rooms, etc. The emotional description of a house includes words that make readers feel something about the house. Before you write an emotional description, you must decide what emotion you want your readers to feel. Do you want your readers to love the house or hate it? Or would you like your readers to feel frightened by the house? Once you decide on the emotional response you want, think of some words that will make readers feel the right emotion. Think of ways you can combine those words with the facts about the house to complete your description.

WRITE

Write two descriptions of the same house, one factual and the other emotional. Before you start writing, picture the house clearly in your mind. Then write a factual description of what you see. Finally, use the same facts to write the emotional description.

_____

_____

_____

(continue on another sheet of paper)

The Proper Time And Place

OH, MOM!

THINK

Think about how many ways you can say the words, "Oh, Mom." Try saying them as if you were angry, surprised, happy, scared, or sad. The meaning comes from the way you say the words.

In writing, words must express emotions without anyone there to say them the right way. The writer must choose words carefully in order to create the emotional response he or she wants. Choose the wrong word and the mood or emotion is sure to be ruined.

What is wrong with this description?

> Nancy came running in from the barn. Her eyes were shining with happiness. "Oh, Mom," she grunted, "he's beautiful."

Clearly, the word "grunted" is the wrong one to describe Nancy's speech. It destroys the mood of the event. Would one of these fit better: "gasped," "whispered," "yelled," "shrieked," "mumbled," or "cooed"? Several would make sense, and each one would show Nancy in a little different way.

The good writer knows when to use emotion and when to avoid it. When emotion is needed, the writer selects words carefully to create the right response.

WRITE

Pick one of these situations, and write a paragraph about it. Describe the situation from the point of view of one character, and try to make your readers feel the same emotion your character feels.

> Ray just got his first job. He must deliver his newspapers every morning at 5 a.m. When he tells his mother about the job, she is not as pleased as Ray expected.

> Janet received an invitation to Bob's birthday party. She told Ann about it, but Ann had not received an invitation.

> Tammy didn't have her homework. She told the teacher that her older brother had taken it by mistake. The teacher punished Tammy by giving her an extra assignment to do.

(continue on another sheet of paper)

Dear Ann Landers:

THINK

Every day, all over the United States, people read advice columns in their daily newspapers. The columns consist of letters from men and women with problems, followed by brief answers from the advice columnist. The letters are often filled with emotion. But they must also be realistic or else they won't appear in the newspaper.

Think about a family problem you have observed. It could be an argument, how one member of the family treats another, or a lack of understanding between parents and children. You can use your own family situation, a family you know well, or you can create an imaginary family with a problem.

Decide which character is going to send the letter, and develop the situation from that person's point of view. What would he or she complain about? What help would this person need? What advice would he or she ask for?

WRITE

Write a letter to the well-known advice columnist, Ann Landers. In your letter describe the family situation from your character's viewpoint. Tell how he or she feels about the others involved. Include a specific example that shows the problem in the family. Ask for help in deciding what to do, how to act, and what to say. Use colorful and emotional words so that Ann Landers and her readers will see the situation clearly and feel involved in it.

Remember to change all the names and to keep your letter serious. A silly letter will be ignored. When you're finished, go back and read your letter again. Make sure that the entire letter takes your character's point of view and that it presents good reasons for needing advice.

Dear Ann Landers:

_____

_____

_____

_____

_____

_____

_____

(continue on another sheet of paper)

Dear Sir:

THINK

To be effective, a business letter needs to present the facts. A letter that is filled with emotion but short on facts is often not taken seriously. If you are applying for a job, selling something, or complaining about a product or service, you want your reader to take you seriously. You must be able to write a business letter that states the facts clearly.

WRITE

Pick one of the following situations. Write a clear and factual business letter to the appropriate person. Try to keep your emotions out of your letter. At the same time, try to be as convincing as you can. You want your letter to produce results!

A waitress dropped a piece of chocolate pie into your lap, but she refused to admit it was her fault. Your expensive white pants were ruined! Write a letter of complaint to the national headquarters of the restaurant chain.

You ordered a shirt from a catalog. You wanted to give the shirt as a birthday present, but it took six months to arrive. When it finally came, it was the wrong color and the wrong size, and it had a big hole in the sleeve. Write a letter to send back with the shirt. Tell the catalog company what you think of its service, its product, and the difference between what it advertises and what it delivers.

You see a help-wanted ad in the newspaper for a delivery person. The ad tells you to send a letter in order to apply for the job. You decide you want the job. Write a letter that will convince the company that you are the right one to hire.

You have decided to sell your collection of comic books (or any other type of collection). In response to your ad in the newspaper, someone writes to ask about your collection. Convince the person in your letter of reply that your collection is really worth buying.

Dear _____ ,

_____

_____

(continue on another sheet of paper)

You Should Have Been There!

THINK

When you tell a friend about something exciting, your voice shows your excitement. When you write a letter about something exciting, you can make your words sound exciting, too.

Think about ways you can put excitement into your sentences and paragraphs.

WRITE

The big building across the street from where you live caught fire last night. The whole inside of the building was filled with flames. Firemen fought the blaze for hours before bringing it under control. Some firemen got hurt. You were awake most of the night because your house was in danger.

Your best friend is away visiting relatives. Write a letter that tells your friend all about the fire, your feelings that night, and what the burned-out building looks like now. Remember, this is a letter to your *best friend*, so let your feelings show.

Dear _____ ,

_____

_____

_____

_____

_____

_____

_____

_____

_____

_____

(continue on another sheet of paper)

A Reporter's Job

THINK

News reporters describe events, but they try to keep their personal feelings out of their reporting. These reporters go to the scene of accidents, fires, and natural disasters. They tell what caused the event, how it happened, and the final result.

WRITE

The big building across the street from your house burned last night. The whole inside of the building was filled with flames. You were awake most of the night because your house was in danger. Many firemen fought the blaze before bringing it under control. Some were hurt.

You are a reporter. Since you were an eyewitness at the fire, your editor assigns you to write a report. What will you say? What are the important facts to include? Be sure to keep your personal feelings out of the report. Your editor wants "the facts and only the facts."

Four-Alarm Fire Guts Warehouse On Main Street

_____

_____

_____

_____

_____

_____

_____

_____

_____

(continue on another sheet of paper)

Disaster

THINK

EARTHQUAKE FLATTENS L.A.
FLOODS WASH AWAY ROADS AND CROPS
HOMES DESTROYED BY TORNADO

Headlines like these often appear on the front page of a newspaper. The articles under the headlines usually describe natural disasters in an unemotional, factual way.

Think about a natural disaster and the people and places it harms. Look at news reports about similar events to get ideas. Make a list of the destructive things that occur, using descriptive — but unemotional — words to tell what happened.

Damaging Effects of the Disaster

WRITE

Use your list to write an objective newspaper article about the disaster. Tell what happened, but do not include any personal feelings. Stick to the facts and avoid emotions.

_____

_____

_____

_____

(continue on another sheet of paper)

Thank Heaven

THINK

Reread your disaster article, and then picture a family who survived the destruction. Think about the way they felt as the disaster unfolded. Think about the people they met and the heroic deeds they saw. Finally, think about their hopes and plans for the future.

Make a list of words and phrases that you can use to express the family's feelings during and after the disaster. Be sure to include descriptive words that are vivid and emotional.

List of Key Emotional Words

WRITE

Using the factual article you wrote for "Disaster" as background information, write an article that tells a personal story about a family of survivors. You want your readers to feel the emotions of the situation, not just know the facts. Use vivid words and descriptions to make the family's fears and joys come alive for your readers.

One Family That Survived

_____

_____

_____

_____

_____

(continue on another sheet of paper)